A RELUCTANT FUNERAL DIRECTOR

David Rymer

MINERVA PRESS

ATLANTA LONDON SYDNEY

ISBN 0 75410 574 1

First Published 1998 by
MINERVA PRESS
Sixth Floor
Canberra House
315–317 Regent Street
London W1R 7YB

Printed in Great Britain for Minerva Press

A RELUCTANT
FUNERAL DIRECTOR

To my father, Jack,
for his vision and commitment.

Chapter One

'What are we going to do with him now, Jack?'

These ominous words were uttered by the Reverend Reg Bainton to my father, Jack Rymer, funeral director, and referred to me and my imminent discharge from The Royal Marines School of Music at Deal in Kent. I do not think anyone else present that day would have ever told me, but my grandmother Ella, my mother's mother, happened to be there and, probably unknown to Reg, my father's friend, did not take kindly to anything being said that was detrimental or might possibly imply that I was already a failure at such an early age. This consultation took place in the autumn of 1955 and it was some years later when Ella divulged its comments to me.

I had quite an undistinguished time at school, taking an instant dislike to it from my first day at Clifton Preparatory School, York. The only thing worth recording was that Judi Dench, destined to become a celebrated actress, was there at the same time. Judi must have been quite an actress even then, because on my first day at school, my mother and Miss Meaby, the Principal, were virtually trying to drag me through the front gate, such was my aversion to the place, and were having little success. Judi then appeared and managed to persuade me that it was not really such a bad place. I meekly entered the gate resigned to my fate. My mother never forgot how kind she had been to me and followed her career with great interest.

My next two schools were Tang Hall Primary and – after my failing to get a scholarship – Burnholme Secondary Modern. It was towards the end of my time there that my future was discussed. As I have already mentioned, my academic record was less than brilliant, so of course this narrowed the options. One thing I knew for sure was I did not want to be a funeral director; and the only thing I can recall having any enthusiasm for was the Merchant Navy. I do not think I would have ended up Master of one of the *Queens* but I would hopefully have seen something of the world at a much earlier age than I did. I remember visiting the careers officer with my mother and father and being steered away from that idea. The man then suggested a compromise. I had been a chorister and a pianist from quite an early age, receiving piano lessons from Peggy Hurst, a very patient teacher. Although I was not the most talented pianist in the world I was not the worst, and the careers man suggested the Royal Marines School of Music. This is where musicians are trained for land based military bands. The school also trains musicians and buglers who serve on Royal Navy ships; so if the careers man got his way, I would become a seagoing pianist. Everyone thought this was a good idea; I was not so sure.

Anyway, entrance examinations had to be passed and my track record was not good. In due course I went to Hull for the general education examination, to Manchester for a medical, and finally to Liverpool for a music examination. For part of the examination I had to play a classical piece of my own choice. Peggy Hurst, my music teacher, decided on Beethoven's *Für Elise*. I practised this for many weeks, then went to Liverpool for the examination. This took place in a large building. I remember a wide staircase, at the top of which was a large hall where I had to wait. When my turn came I was ushered into a spacious room where two men were waiting. In the middle of the room was a very imposing grand piano, the first I had played. Peggy had one in her room but it was only a baby grand and I was never allowed to play it; I was confined to the upright. The two examiners asked me several questions, which I presume were part of the examination, then on to Beethoven's *Für Elise*. I have to say I think I gave a virtually flawless performance. I do not think there was one wrong note – a credit to Peggy Hurst and hours of practice. Several weeks later I was informed that I had passed: a surprise to everyone.

I arrived in Deal in May, 1955, via one night at the YWCA, Manchester. Yes, that is correct, Young *Women's* Christian Association – quite an experience. I think I had been in Deal about four days when I realised that a Royal Marine Bandsman's career was not for me. The first thing we did was embark on parade training, what I could only call toughening up training. This involved rope climbing, crawling through pipes, cross-country running, canoeing in the English Channel and trying to keep afloat with a full pack on our backs. Luckily, this was done in a swimming pool, and it was all right if you were a good swimmer. I was, but if you weren't, like one or two of the participants you just about drowned. After this training came the music. I think I am correct in saying that everyone had to play a second instrument; certainly pianists did, for the obvious reasons. I, to my great disappointment, was allocated the flute. It's a wonderful instrument but not for me. The worst thing of all was I had to start from scratch and what I would have liked was the trumpet or saxophone; no such luck. Part of every day was filled by attending classes to continue our conventional education; all the teachers were naval officers. The rest of the day was taken up with music tuition, some of it for the flute, other days the piano. In charge of the piano tuition was Professor Bixter. He operated in a building four or five storeys high with probably four or five rooms on each floor, each containing a piano. Every pianist would spend maybe two or three hours alone in a room practising, and then some time during the week had a lesson with Professor Bixter.

So this was it: going to school, playing the piano in solitude and trying to learn to play an instrument I disliked. Within two months, probably less, I was beginning to suffer from acute boredom and, I expect, homesickness. The highlight of the day was a visit to the NAAFI on an evening or a visit to the cinema at the weekend which, as I recall, was within the barracks perimeter. Later, when we had completed our parade training, we were able to walk into Deal on some evenings and at weekends; but it was becoming increasingly obvious that this was not the life for me. I expect the first indication my family had of my feelings would come from the frequent letters I sent them. During the summer, my mother and sister, Christine, spent a weekend at Deal, and before they left I do not think there was any doubt in their minds that I wanted out.

Some time after their return I had a telephone conversation with my father. He asked me to stay a little longer to make absolutely sure that this career was not for me. This 'little longer' was about two weeks and I then confirmed to my parents that my decision was irrevocable. However, to get a discharge from the Royal Marines School of Music you have to have a valid reason. After some time it was decided that I had come to the conclusion that I wanted to enter the family business. There was an element of truth in this. To escape the life I was now leading, I think I would have entered anything provided there was not a flute there.

During the course of the discharge I had to go before the Commanding Officer, Major MacLeod, so he could make sure I was not making a mistake. I do not think I was terribly convincing because I remember him asking me,

'Are you sure you want to be an undertaker?' 'Yes, I am sure,' I replied. There was a look of incredulity on his face.

So in November, 1955, the blessed day of my discharge came. My father having paid the £50 buying out fee, I left Deal with my kitbag containing what things were deemed to be mine, a spare pair of boots, clothes brush, etc., and a railway pass for my return to York. I wore my uniform for the last time; that had to be returned to Deal when I got home.

Did I gain any benefits by my short stay in Deal? I think so. They turned me into an athlete, which was something probably lying just under the surface at school but never quite able to emerge. I acquired some swimming qualifications – as far as I am aware the only qualifications I possess. I learnt the real meaning of discipline, and it does not do anyone any harm to experience this at least once in his or her life; and finally for a short time I was a member of in my view the finest military band in this country and probably the world. I was not the only prospective bandsman to leave the Royal Marines School of Music. Others did as well; some who were older than me were able to transfer to the Royal Marines for a career without music. Would I have done that if I could? Who knows? The idea certainly appealed to me at the time.

Chapter Two

Before I start to recall my early days in the funeral profession I would like to look back at how it all started for the Rymer family. Up until 1848 my family lived and worked at Coxwold, a village twenty miles north of York. The most famous previous inhabitant of Coxwold was Laurence Sterne, the eighteenth-century Irish-born novelist and clergyman. His home, Shandy Hall, still stands near the church and can be visited by the public.

James Rymer, who was born in 1813, was my great-great grandfather. He was a joiner and as far as I am aware had no early connection with funerals. One of his main customers was a property owner and it appears that James used to repair and maintain his property. This man subsequently bought considerable property in York. James decided that this was where his business future lay and, in what must in those days have seemed like emigrating, moved lock, stock and barrel to York. He bought a house in St Andrewgate within a few hundred yards of York Minster, with enough land at the rear to construct a workshop. The first few years he worked for the property owner and at the same time started to build up some work with private customers, mainly consisting of repairs to numerous small shops in streets surrounding St Andrewgate including the renowned Shambles about fifty yards away. His old ledgers, which we still have, make interesting reading.

James's first connection with any funeral was, sadly, that of his own daughter Margaret, who fell ill and died in

August, 1854. The reason he decided to arrange the funeral instead of asking another undertaker is not clear; it might have been cost – there were certainly times when business was not good – or maybe he thought already being a joiner he would make the coffin himself and continue with the funeral arrangements. However, that is how it appears to have started and from then on funeral accounts start to appear in the ledgers among other miscellaneous joinery work. Sometimes they are several months apart.

In the next few years James acquired some more property, and the funerals gradually increased. Nothing of great note was recorded in the succeeding years. James and Martha had several children, at least two of them dying at a very early age. James's son, also James, entered the business and worked with his father, and although I cannot say for sure I think James senior played quite a prominent role in the business, even in his later years. It has been passed down through the family that he was once describe conducting a funeral, when he was turned eighty, as being tall and erect. James died in 1898, aged eighty-five years. He lived longer than any known male member of the Rymer family so far. James junior then ran the business until his death in 1914, to be succeeded by his eldest son John, my grandfather.

John had two brothers, Robert and Reginald, neither of whom wished to be involved in the business. They were a couple of flamboyant characters and there are various stories about these two. One such story handed down recalls Bob and Reg, as young boys, smoking in bed on the top floor of the house in St Andrewgate when they managed to set the bed on fire. Bob rushed downstairs to get some water and on his way back up with a bucketful of water was confronted by James, his grandfather.

'Where are you going with that, Bob?' he said.

A terrified Bob responded, 'Our Reg wants a drink of water.'

Bob Wright, of William Wright, the well-known York butchers, was a friend of Uncle Bob and in later years would recall to me some for the things they used to get up to in those early days. This included once riding one of Wright's horses around the yard in Aldwark, York, till the unfortunate creature expired; not something to be proud of.

Towards the end of the Boer War of 1899–1902, both Bob and Reg lied about their age and enlisted in the army. Both survived the war unscathed. Reg remaining as a regular soldier for some years, spending time in York whenever he could. He eventually married and ended up living in London, where he died some time just after the Second World War. Bob embarked on several enterprises, one of which subsequently terminated his business career in York. He became a carriage master, owning several carriages and horses. He operated from a yard and stable in Ogleforth, close to Monk Bar, the old eastern gate entrance to the city. Some of the carriages were suitable enough to be hired to funeral directors and were involved in J. Rymer Funerals. It seems that brother Reg must have helped him sometimes, probably when on leave. One day he was driving one of the carriages in St Saviourgate and was in collision with a council steamroller. No one was injured but legal action followed when it transpired that Reg had indulged in some measure of alcohol prior to the collision. There were no breathalysers in those days, but virtually the same result. Damages were awarded and it was enough to finish Bob and his business.

My grandfather continued to run his business until 1925 when he was suddenly struck with an illness. My father told me that it was strongly suspected that he had con- tracted the disease from one of his clients, although this was never proved and would not have made any difference anyway. My grandfather died within a very short time. My father was fifteen and was already working for the firm, and my grandmother decided to try and continue running the business, although she had virtually no administrative experience. They continued for about eighteen months by this time the business was in some financial difficulty.

A family conference ensued which probably consisted of my grandmother, father and my father's sister, Nancy. There were no other brothers or sisters. My grandmother asked my father if he wanted to continue with the business. My father said he would on the condition he had sole charge of everything, and this was agreed. He would continue with the joinery work including the making of coffins, and the administration. Harold Dixon, a funeral director with his own business and a friend of my grandfather, offered to arrange and conduct the funerals until my father was able to continue himself.

It is extremely unlikely that the funeral side of the business would have been sustained without Harold's help, and indeed my father often mentioned the debt of gratitude he owed Harold Dixon. Father probably arranged and conducted his first funeral when he was seventeen; he was still very young but during the time Harold was there he was learning all the time. By the time he was eighteen he was on his own. The business debts had been paid off and although it was quite a struggle for some time, eventually the business started to prosper. He had help from his uncles George and Ted, my grandmother's brothers. Towards the end of the 1920s, Harry Cook came to work for my father and remained for over fifty years; I will return to Harry later.

My father met my mother, Audrey, sometime in the mid 1930s. Her address was Cemetery Road. They were married in 1939 and bought a house in Broadway West, Fulford. I was born in 1940. By this time, of course, the

War had started and my grandmother was living on her own at St Andrewgate. My Father travelled to work from Fulford on his bike. It was decided, and very reluctantly so by my mother, that due to the War, with blackouts and the likelihood of air raids, they should leave Broadway West and move to St Andrewgate. I do not think my mother ever got over leaving a modern semi-detached house for a very old and cold four-storey unmodernised Georgian house.

It was in 1942, I think, that my father was ordered to report to the recruitment centre in York, and after interviews and medicals he was told that he would he joining the Fleet Air Arm and that he would be called up in due course. My father then had to work fast. The problem was how the business could survive in his absence. Coffins had to be made and funerals arranged and conducted. My father was friendly with Dick Thornton, who was a director of Fairweather's, the joiners, in Spen Lane, the next street to St Andrewgate. He arranged with Dick to make the coffins, while my father's brother-in-law, Tom Oliver, who was the funeral director at Whitby C. Oliver of Micklegate, York, agreed to arrange and conduct the funerals. So while my father awaited his call-up he carried on with the business – but the call never came. He was never absolutely sure why he was not called to the colours but his cousin, Edwin Rymer was; he was convinced that he was called up by mistake instead of my father. Edwin had taken a medical but had not passed anything like A1. Edwin spent his time in the London Fire Service and, in his own words, spent the War being 'blown up and down the Thames'. So for the duration of the War my father ran his business arranging and conducting his funerals but did not make the coffins. He was also a part-time fireman and a member of the mortuary squad, which was formed to recover victims of air raids. This as you can imagine was a quite traumatic job and funeral directors were very suitable for this task.

My own personal memory of the War was mainly of the air raids; we had our Anderson air raid shelter in the garden, and our friends the Dunn family who lived a few doors from us had an indoor Morrison shelter. I think we must have used our Anderson shelter at the beginning of the War and the Morrison shelter later. When the air raid siren was sounded, grandma, my father's mother and I were the first occupants of the shelter; then the others followed later, including on some occasions neighbours. Inside the shelter there were wooden chairs; the Morrison shelter was far comfier and warmer and had beds made up inside.

My only other clear memory of the War was one Sunday when my father and his friend Bill Dunn took Bill junior and myself to the river at Poppleton on bikes. While we were playing there, a German plane flew past us so low that you could see the pilot. It was thought he was using the river to find his way back to the coast and when he got to York he dropped a bomb, which I think landed in Skeldergate. A friend of mine, Andrew Brodie, who also lived in St Andrewgate, was in St George's Field just across the river from Skeldergate and remembers the incident clearly.

On the 11th August, 1940, a bomb landed in York Cemetery, badly damaging the military memorial, which was later replaced. Many headstones were also damaged and this is still quite evident today. My maternal grandmother was living, as I have already said, in Cemetery Road, about fifty yards from where the bomb dropped. Her house and many others sustained quite heavy damage, although as far as I am aware no one was seriously injured.

Chapter Three

During the War the funeral side of the business had gradually increased. My father then found it difficult to operate the joinery work and funerals side by side. The problem with funerals is you never know when they are coming, and when they do everything else has to be put on hold. So if my father had started, say, repairing a shop front he would be expected to continue until it was completed. If then a funeral came in, he had to stop for so long to make the arrangements and then make the coffin and then conduct the funeral. If he had, say, three funerals at the same time, he had a problem. So he decided it had to be one or the other – property repairs or funerals – and he chose funerals. This was quite a decision to make. If funerals on their own could not sustain the business, by the time this became evident the joinery customers would be established elsewhere.

So, for the first time, J. Rymer were exclusively funeral directors. It was a struggle at first, but gradually the business grew. Except for the period when Bob Rymer supplied the business with horse-drawn coaches and carriages, the business hired from various carriage masters. The first one my father was involved with was 'Robby' – I am not sure of his full name. In those days the funeral director walked in front of the hearse from the house in cortège to the church and finally to the cemetery. After the interment had taken place the funeral director would ride back to the house on top of the first coach which contained the immediate family. His seat would be beside the coach driver. My father said that Robby was the only one on a wet day who would cover his seat with his cloak so that when my father sat down he was not in a pool of water.

My father recalled an incident when he was walking in front of the hearse in cortège. His sister, Nancy, was walking my father's dog and as the cortège approached the dog stopped and took a good long look at my father. It could not make its mind up if it was him then all of a sudden it realised it was and was into the road jumping up at him. By the time Nancy got to the dog the funeral had for a minute or two lost a little dignity.

The first mention in our ledgers of any motorised conveyance appeared in 1918, when the business hired a motor hearse for a removal from Beverley Asylum to York. Any removals of any distance prior to that date would have had to be in a horse-drawn hearse which most probably would have been a day's job. At that time most people died at home and remained there until the day of the funeral. There were no chapels of rest. When the coffin was made, the undertaker and one of his men would carry it on their shoulders through the streets to the house. This must have been a common enough sight in those days. The first mention I can find of a motor hearse being used for a funeral was June, 1925. The lady who died was Harriet Wrigley and the funeral took place at Stillingfleet, a village about six miles south of York.

It would appear that horse-drawn and motor hearses ran side by side for quite a few years. The family were probably asked their preference when the funeral was being arranged. I cannot find a mention in our ledger of a horse-drawn hearse or cab being used after 1938, so it seems that J. Rymer were using motor hearses and limousines exclusively by the outbreak of World War II, although I cannot say for certain whether horse-drawn funeral vehicles were not still being mainly used by other funeral directors.

I must just mention to you one story my father told me which occurred during the transition period. It became quite a problem when carriage masters began to transfer from horse to motor; the cab driver had to be taught to drive motor cars, and this was quite a big thing for someone to do after a working life driving horses. One day they were giving one of the cab drivers a driving lesson and it was not going too well as they approached a busy crossroads where he was told to brake. He immediately took a firmer grip of the steering wheel and shouted, 'Whoo!'

For some years preceding the War, and until 1945, my father was hiring his vehicles from Alf Dalton, the carriage master who lived on the Mount. I understand he had what was formerly his stables, and became his garage, in Dalton Terrace, which links The Mount with Holgate Road. Jim Hudson, a York funeral director who is about fifteen years older than me, tells me he is fairly sure that is how Dalton Terrace got its name. I understand Alf and my father became friends and would enjoy a pint or two together on many occasions. Alf became ill and died in January, 1945. My father was given the opportunity to purchase Alf's fleet and he did so but he could not afford the garage. That immediately created the problem of where to garage four large vehicles. The fleet consisted of a 1928 Rolls-Royce hearse and two limousines, an Austin and Humber. I think the other vehicle was a Standard. He managed to acquire a large garage on lease in Hungate, just off St Saviourgate, overlooking where Stonebow now is.

At that time in York there were no businesses that were exclusively funeral directors. I think J. Rymer was the first. The funeral directors hired their vehicles from the carriage masters and these where James Walker in Clarence Street, Scobey's in Bootham and Outhwaites in Acomb and now

J. Rymer. This caused resentment which lasted a few years and certainly in those early days there was not much chance of one funeral director hiring vehicles from another funeral director. My father, as far as York was concerned, had created a brand new breed, a fully independent funeral director who made his own coffins, arranged and conducted the funeral and now owned his own fleet. I think by now you will have realised that the relationship, certainly between some of the funeral directors, was less than friendly and virtually all Alf Dalton's customers dispersed to the other carriage masters, with the exception of one or two who probably owed money to the business and decided it was easier to remain.

Over the next few years the business gradually prospered. The funerals increased and some of the other funeral directors started to hire vehicles off my father. However, if he had a quiet period – and once he went two weeks without a funeral – it was quite worrying, as this was the only income the business had.

My father then began to think of some way he could supplement his income, particularly with the fleet in mind. A hearse is definitely a one-purpose vehicle. It was then and still is today. It conveys a coffin during the course of a funeral and that is it. You have a bit more opportunity with limousines. At first he acquired work carrying things rather than people. He obtained a contract with a small laundry at Haxby collecting and delivering laundry baskets, and then another contract with a local dance band taking the instruments, including drums, to different venues and then returning them afterwards.

It was about this time that we started hiring out limousines for weddings.

Even today, most funeral directors who own a fleet are very likely to hire out their limousines for weddings. Most of them will also be involved with chauffeur drive. We probably did our first 'private hire' as it was then known in the mid-Fifties, and this is where I come in: November, 1955, to be precise.

Chapter Four

My first day at J. Rymer was a mixture of relief and apprehension; relief that I was not any longer a Marine Bandsman but apprehension at embarking on a career I never wanted to be involved with, although I had no comprehension then of how long it was to last.

Our business premises at 35, St Andrewgate, consisted of a four-storey house. At the rear of the building was a long garden and at the end of the garden was a large workshop, elevated about ten feet from the ground; and underneath the workshop was a large timber store. The workshop had four workbenches, a circular saw, a planer, sanding machines and an electric drill: all very necessary equipment for the manufacture of coffins. The house had to double as an office. There was the lounge known all my life as the front room. This was our office. The only window looked out on to St Andrewgate and in this room all the administration work took place. This was also where families were able to come and arrange a funeral.

There was no rear access to the premises, so everything and everybody had to come through the front door. There was a long hall from the front door which led right through to the garden. It was always known as the passage, well named. So families arranging funerals came through this door, and so did all the materials that were required for the workshop, including large orders of timber sets for the construction of coffins. All the drivers and bearers had to congregate there prior to a funeral, drinking tea in my mother's living room. The consequence of this was very little private life for us during the day.

When I arrived at J. Rymer, I was only the third full-time member of staff, the others being my father and Harry Cook, who when he eventually retired had been with us for over fifty years, with the exception of service during World War II. Harry was like one of the family, and my sister, Christine, and I had never known St Andrewgate when he had not been there.

Harry's main work was in the workshop making coffins. They were usually all English elm in those days. That was our standard coffin; English elm had succeeded pitch pine coffins some years before. The more lavish funeral involved either solid oak, which could be English, American or Japanese oak, or maybe chestnut. The majority of the English elm coffins were polished to a dark colour with two coats of button polish and then finished with one coat of shellac varnish. Polishing was Harry's speciality, and in time I became a quite competent polisher myself, largely thanks to what I learnt from Harry.

If the deceased's family had chosen a solid oak coffin and wanted it dark, then we would call in the services of Wallace Martin, who was an excellent french polisher. Wallace and his father before him had been polishing coffins for J. Rymer for many years. On the day they were coming, the workshop had to have a high temperature and the coffin had to be sandpapered to a glass-like surface. If either of these prerequisites were not met, Wallace would not start work. He was indeed a perfectionist. The alternative to a dark finish coffin was a wax finish. Wax was put on the coffin then rubbed off; not a lot of skill required there. Incidentally, Wallace Martin was the man who was responsible for me becoming a chorister. He was a long serving member of the St Maurice church choir in Monkgate, York – now no longer there – and suggested to my parents that I went for an audition. I expect this probably had something to do with me becoming a pianist, so maybe Wallace had more of an influence on my life than he ever realised. In his later years he was custodian and churchwarden of Holy Trinity Church, Goodramgate, York, and there is a bench in the churchyard to commemorate him.

My first two years or so were spent doing various tasks, making tea, sweeping the workshop floor, which was always covered in wood shavings, and cleaning the hearse and the cars. The 1928 Rolls-Royce hearse required the most attention. It was a very high vehicle and to clean its roof and flower rail required standing on a box to reach the very top. The famous radiator front with the Spirit of Ecstasy was made of German silver and required cleaning every day with Brasso, and if it rained between funerals, maybe two or three times. For some reason which I was never quite sure of, we could not put antifreeze in the radiator, so in winter each night it had to be drained and the next morning filled. I was never sure how much water its enormous radiator held, but it would take Harry and myself about twenty to twenty-five minutes to fill with two watering cans. It never had a petrol gauge so we had to keep a check on how many miles it had done so that we would know when to refuel, and of course it never had a heater. On cold winter days I am sure it was colder inside the hearse than outside.

It was at about this time that we found we were unable to renew the lease of our large garage in Hungate, so Father had to try and find a new garage. It proved impossible to find a garage which would accommodate all the vehicles, but we managed to lease two covered garage spaces alongside Mrs Dunford's house in St Andrewgate and some time later two more spaces alongside Sam Jackson's house, also in St Andrewgate.

Without doubt the hardest job for my father was trying to teach me to make coffins. A joiner I was not; my woodwork teacher at Burnholme School, Mr Eccles, had once remarked that he hoped I was not going into the family business. He thought my ability as a joiner was less than adequate to construct a coffin. I remember my father once buying me a fretwork set for my birthday or Christmas and being bitterly disappointed when I discovered what it was. So I think it is fair to say that I was not a natural; the first work I did on coffins was mainly sandpapering, the most simple of jobs and also quite boring. My father then bought me my own set of joinery tools; wood planers, chisels and hammers (two required for coffins). He had more confidence than me, but as time went on I progressed into the actual construction of coffins; and there must be some truth in the maxim that if you do something for long enough, you get good at it. After about three years, I could make a good coffin. I do not think I could have made anything else, but I never tried, so who knows? All we ever made in our workshop was exclusively coffins.

By 1957 the business had expanded to the extent that we were badly in need of more space. We wanted to increase the number of vehicles in our fleet but were unable to find any more suitable garage space. Still more important was the extra space we required for storing coffins. We also needed a Chapel of Rest. More people were now dying in hospital rather than at home and the tradition of people having their deceased relatives in their house until the day of the funeral was declining.

Our premises at 35, St Andrewgate, were part of a block of three houses. Around about this time numbers 33 and 31 became unsafe, and in a very short period of time the families were rehoused and both the properties demolished. This left quite a large space which my father was able to lease from York Corporation as a car park. He then attempted to purchase the land with a view to expanding our existing premises but was unsuccessful. I am fairly sure that by this time Lord Esher's plan to return parts of the old City close within the City walls to residential property had been accepted, and this meant that any businesses which could be encouraged to move out of this area would go. In fact, within a few years all the businesses in the St Andrewgate area had been relocated in other parts of the city.

My father then decided that we must look for a house as near to St Andrewgate as possible, move there and then use St Andrewgate solely as business premises. At that time my father had no intention of leaving St Andrewgate altogether. We found a large house for sale in Penley's Grove Street and bought it. After some improvements and alterations we moved in; the year was 1958. This meant for the first time since 1848 no one was actually living on the business premises. Up until that time someone had always been there to answer the door or the telephone, the same theory applying then as it still does today that when someone dies the family want and deserves immediate attention from the funeral director.

With us now living at Penley's Grove Street we were able to concentrate on converting all of St Andrewgate to business premises. What had been our living room at St Andrewgate would, we decided, become our Chapel of Rest. It was already a wood panelled room, so all we needed to do was construct an altar of the same wood panelling over the fireplace, and we had a very natural looking chapel.

We were now able to accept agencies from two coffin manufacturers. This meant we would store coffins on their behalf to supply to other funeral directors in our area. What had been two bedrooms on the first floor became coffin stores. We also made an area under the workshop into a store. This gave us capacity to store about two hundred and fifty standard veneered coffins.

We still made solid timber coffins ourselves, but not now having to make the majority of coffins ourselves gave us much more time to concentrate on the other aspects of the business. What had been our front room/lounge/office now became a full-time office. My father already had his bureau there and we now added an extra desk for me. But in spite of all the extra space we now had, the exterior of the building looked almost derelict. This of course was largely due to the demolition of 31 and 33, St Andrewgate, but we did have for the first time premises that were used exclusively for business.

Chapter Five

In April, 1958, I passed my driving test (on the second attempt). This immediately increased my usefulness to the business, which now had two full-time drivers, Father and myself. Within a very short period of time I was driving cars on funerals and conveying families who had no transport to the registrar. By this time our 1928 Rolls-Royce hearse was sadly over the hill, in fact well down the other side, not mechanically but, for want of another word, 'bodily'.

Up until this time motor hearses had been large and ornate but now some of the coachbuilders who specialised in building hearses and limousines where looking to build these vehicles on a smaller chassis. Of course, one obvious advantage was the cost. To build a hearse on a Rolls-Royce chassis against a chassis from a standard production model made a considerable difference. Woodhall Nicholson, the coachbuilders at Halifax, built a hearse on an Austin Cambridge chassis. The end result was a much smaller hearse, well in proportion, and it had dignity and style. Of course, when anything new comes along it seems a natural reaction for some to criticise; but Father took a chance as he was able to buy a new hearse at a price he could afford. Within a year we sold the Rolls-Royce hearse. We understand that it was scrapped but the engine survived and was used to power an aircraft. If that is true, I wonder if the people in the aircraft ever knew about its original use.

Around about this time we bought our first Humber Pullman limousine. It was second-hand and had been the director's car at Brightsteels, Malton. This was an ideal car for our profession. We now were able to sell our ageing Vauxhall.

As I have mentioned previously, the limousines were used for weddings and at about this time we became more involved in chauffeur drive; this was mainly for American tourists but sometimes businessmen required chauffeur-driven cars. A national rail strike would very often mean a limousine was required to convey some businessmen or business lady from York to a meeting or appointment which could not be missed.

One day I had to meet an American air force colonel at York Station and 'drive as directed', dreaded terminology for a chauffeur. The concern is that they are going to ask to be conveyed somewhere you have never heard of. Anyway, I arrived at York Station and still being rather naive in those days expected to see a colonel in full dress uniform emerge from the station concourse. Of course when I did meet him he was in civilian clothes. He asked me to drive to Pickering, a small town at the southern end of the North York Moors. When we arrived there we stopped at The Forest and Vale Hotel, which I would think is the largest hotel in Pickering. He remained there long enough to leave his suitcase and then he asked me to drive on the A169 road towards Whitby which traverses the North York Moors. After we had travelled approximately twelve miles from Pickering, he asked me to slow down as we were going to turn right fairly soon. As I looked round I realised we could not have been in a more remote area; there was not a building or person in sight, just what seemed endless miles of moorland. He then said we will be turning right in about two hundred yards. When we finally arrived at the turning it was virtually a dirt track, fairly level and no potholes, but still something that looked only suitable for tractors. By this time I was beginning to wonder what the colonel had in mind, as far as I could see the track, appeared to lead nowhere. When we had travelled what seemed to be a considerable distance from the road he said please stop here and wait! He then climbed out of the car and closed the door.

After a moment or two I turned and looking over my left shoulder and there in the middle of the moors and miles from anywhere was an enormous hole in the ground, the entrance and the tunnel beyond brightly lit by what seemed very strong fluorescent lights. Something told me to remain in the car. After about an hour maybe more the colonel returned. I drove him back to The Forest and Vale, and nothing was said. That day I had taken the colonel to Fylingdales Moor, the site of the Fylingdales Early Warning Station.

Within maybe a year the famous golf balls had appeared and would remain for the next thirty years as a reminder to us all of the precarious times we then lived in. The following year to eighteen months I made many more journeys to Fylingdales; sometimes there were as many as five or six limousines at a time conveying what I presume were American technicians and army or air force personnel to the Station. None of these, of course, could compete with that first mysterious journey.

In 1961, York had a royal wedding. HRH The Duke of Kent married Miss Katherine Worsley from Hovingham at York Minster. We had cars involved on the day of the ceremony, but my most interesting experience was when I conveyed Sir Cecil Beaton and his colleague to Hovingham to prepare for the royal wedding photographs.

Over the years we built up a considerable number of accounts in chauffeur drive including some well-known personalities. York Races was always quite a busy time for us and we had regular work meeting some of the racehorse owners, who would fly in to either Leeds-Bradford airport, or sometimes to some of the smaller airfields in the York area, in their own private planes. We even had an agent in the USA but there was never enough work in chauffeur drive to warrant adding any more vehicles to the fleet. A similar situation with the weddings. Ninety per cent of weddings are on Saturdays. We could maybe manage three maybe four weddings in a day, and the consequence of this was that we had to refuse as many weddings in the year as we could actually do.

As I mentioned earlier, the only other occasions when we were able to hire our vehicles out were to smaller funeral directors whose businesses were not large enough to warrant their own fleet and where funerals played only a small percentage in the firm's turnover. The ones based in the city often had as their main business joinery contractors, shop owners or house furnishers. Those in the villages round York again could be joinery contractors, sub postmasters and antique dealers, and as far as I am aware the oldest funeral director in the York area is Myers of Wheldrake, dating back to 1725 and still run by the same family. These funeral directors arrange and conduct funerals in the traditional way the local people are used to and they are very unlikely to want the services of larger businesses in the city. In addition to hiring the hearse and limousines they are able to have the use of our Chapel of Rest if the family so wish. On the whole we all enjoy close Cupertino with each other and I will enlarge on this later.

Chapter Six

There are certain circumstances when someone dies which mean the death has to be reported to HM Coroner; some of course are obvious, such as violent or unnatural death. However, the majority of these cases fall into the fourteen-day rule, that is when the doctor has not attended in the last illness or within fourteen days before death. If that person dies at home, the family doctor will report the death to the Coroner and the person must be removed to hospital for a post-mortem to determine the cause of death. Until 1959 all these removals were done in the York Police van which was in fact a black Maria. The York Coroner at that time and for many years previous was Innes Ware. I think over a period of time there had been several complaints by some families into this method of removal, so Mr Ware decided that a more dignified procedure must be found. He approached my father and asked if he would be prepared to remove Coroner cases with a hearse and coffin; we had not progressed to stretchers in those days. My father agreed and in October 1959 we removed our first Coroner's case.

My father was out conducting a funeral in our new Austin Cambridge hearse but we still then had our Rolls-Royce hearse, and that is what the removal was carried out in. I had to go to the address where I met Wilf Jordan, who was the Deputy Coroner's Officer at that time and who subsequently became Coroner's Officer, a post he held for several years. I got to know Wilf fairly well over the years. He made a first class Coroner's Officer, with the ideal manner and temperament for someone whose task is to deal with bereaved people who have lost a member of their family sometimes very suddenly and without warning.

After several weeks it became clear that we were not going to be able to be out of touch with the police for an extended period of time. People do not always die in bed; they sometimes collapse and die where they are, and that can mean in their house, the bathroom or in the garden. If a doctor is called and the death is certified before an ambulance arrives, it becomes a Coroner's removal and any delay then can only cause more distress for the family. My father decided that someone would have to be at or near the office most of the time. This role fell to me and within a few months we were also working for the East Riding and North Riding of Yorkshire Coroners so we became responsible for the City of York and an approximate twenty-mile radius to the north, east and south of York.

When we parted with our Rolls-Royce hearse it was quite obvious that we required an additional vehicle. We then purchased our second new hearse, an Austin Princess Vanden Plas, slightly larger than the Austin Cambridge and very well designed; so the Princess was used for the funerals and the Austin Cambridge remained with me for the removals. It was extremely unlikely in those days to have two funerals at the same time so hopefully our hearse was always available for removals.

I would now like to record that period from 1959 until 1971 when we worked for the three Coroners but first I will give in detail the main circumstances that lead to a death being reported to a Coroner.

The three highest categories that are reported to the Coroner are:

1. The deceased has not seen their doctor within fourteen days of death.

2. The death takes place within twenty-four or forty-eight hours of admission to hospital.

3. Suicide is suspected.

The majority of our removals were from private residences when someone who had become ill had died before they could be admitted to hospital. Maybe the doctor would arrive before the person died; but if the doctor had not seen the patient within fourteen days the death would have to be reported to the Coroner. There could, however, be exceptions if the doctor had been attending the patient and had not seen them for, say, fifteen or sixteen days but was clearly satisfied as to the cause of the death, he would still have to report the death to the Coroner but at the same time expressing his view as to the cause of death. The Coroner then might refer it back to the doctor, who would be asked to issue the death certificate in the normal way.

We sometimes had to remove people who had died as the result of an accident and this could be any sort of accident – industrial, at home, on the water, or in the air involving private planes or gliders. If the accident involved a heavy jet airliner a much larger recovery operation is quite obviously required; but our profession still plays a prominent part, especially the embalmers, who among their other duties assist with recovery and identification; I will elaborate on this work later.

To give some idea of what my work involved in this period working for the Coroners, I would like to recall some of the particular instances, without of course identifying anyone. As I have already said, the majority of deaths reported to the Coroner were from natural causes and the ones I will recall certainly fall into the minority.

Of course any death is a sad occasion for a family, but suicide can have a devastating effect. It might well be that the person has a history of depression or psychiatric illness and has threatened to take their own life. They might have even had previous attempts but when it actually happens it is a horrendous shock. I expect the worst possible instances are when the family discover the person themselves and that sadly is very often the case; the person probably will wait until the rest of the family have left the house, then make the attempt. It may be an overdose of drugs in their bedroom, gassing, exhaust fumes from their own car in the garage, and of course by hanging – in my view the most shocking of them all. It never ceased to amaze me how families managed to come to terms with such tragedy. Sometimes the person will not wait to be alone in the house and will make the attempt while members of the family are present.

Of course being on call for the Coroner meant having to be available twenty-four hours a day. The consequence of this was that whenever I was going out at weekends or at night, I had to leave a contact telephone number. One Saturday afternoon I was attending a family friend's wedding and whilst at the reception I was called away by the Coroner's Officer to a house in York. A young man had returned home, I think from holiday, walked into the house, said hello to his mother gone upstairs and hanged himself. Over the years there were regrettably many similar instances. Not always in the house; they sometimes took place in barns or outhouses in rural areas.

Drowning is also a method which many people choose to take their life. This must be relatively simple if they are non-swimmers, but I have never quite understood how a swimmer walks into a river and drowns unless they are under the influence of alcohol or drugs or have weighted themselves down. This is totally different from someone like Robert Maxwell, who may have jumped or fallen off his yacht at sea and if not missed or picked up by another vessel would eventually die from exhaustion. If that is what actually happened.

I read in the *Yorkshire Evening Press* one night that an American serviceman had been seen jumping off Selby toll bridge into the Ouse. No one had been able to save him and he had quickly disappeared. I remembered thinking to myself, I wonder which direction he will go down – towards Goole or towards York? I knew that if he went towards York, it would be very likely that I would be involved in the recovery. About two months later I received a telephone call from the police in the early hours of the morning informing me that a body had been reported floating near Cawood Bridge and had been secured near the river bank. I immediately asked which bank north or south because my boundary was the north bank, and anything on the south bank came under another Coroner.

Of course it was the north bank. Although I knew there would be at least one police officer there I felt, knowing the circumstances, that I would be happier with some additional help. Harry Cook, who as I have already mentioned worked for us, would always give me a hand out of hours, but I had to go to his house to collect him as he was not on the telephone. But I never went after midnight. So I telephoned my father, woke him up and asked him to come with me. There was no humming and hawing with him, he just asked me how long before I would be picking him up. Cawood Bridge is a swing bridge like Selby Bridge. There is a keeper's hut on the bridge itself and the bridge master lives in the house on the Cawood village bank. The bridge is manned twenty-four hours. I believe it was the keeper who spotted the body.

As we approached the bridge, the police directed us with a lamp to a grassy slope to the side of the bridge. He informed us that the body was several hundred yards down the river towards Selby, certainly too far for us to carry back to the bridge. The only means of getting there was to drive along the top of the flood bank, which was probably only eight feet wide. With the headlights on, this I thought was possible, but the return to the bridge would be considerably harder if I could not turn round on the flood bank.

After a slow and careful drive we arrived at the place on the bank. If someone goes into the water fully clothed, and they usually are, the longer they remain in the water the harder they are to recover. Their clothes become full of thick wet mud making them considerably heavier to lift. This poor unfortunate gentleman was no exception. But what made it worse was he was a giant of a man, and of course he had decomposed. It took three of us some considerable effort to get him up the flood bank and into the removal coffin shell. I then had to decide whether to reverse along the bank, being led by the policeman's lamp, or attempt to turn round. I decided it was too precarious to reverse along the top of this narrow bank in pitch darkness and said I would attempt to turn round. It seemed to take about fifty shunts with the policeman at the rear of the vehicle with his lamp and my father at the front to make sure I did not end up in the river or in the field at the other side – a drop of probably twelve feet. We then lifted the removal shell into the vehicle. The vehicle visibly dropped with the weight. I then drove very slowly and carefully back to the bridge.

The only problem now was to drive up the grassy slope to the road. My first attempt failed halfway up, as did my second, even with some pushing at the rear. I decided that I would have to have a run at it. I reversed to the river's edge then got as much speed up as I could and headed for the slope. As I hit the bottom of the slope and started to climb, there was a loud rending noise from the rear of the hearse but I knew I had to keep going. I only just made it. I got out and with my father and the policeman inspected the hearse. The extra weight in the hearse had caused the hearse to ground as I started to climb and I had parted company with the back bumper, rear foglight and reversing light. It had proved an expensive night's work.

Regrettably, railway lines attract people who decide to take their life either by lying on the track just before the train arrives or sometimes literally walking in front of a train. This is terrible for the victim and his or her family but is also a very traumatic experience for the train driver, who has very little chance of stopping if someone is determined on such a course. Over the years I have removed many victims who ended their life this way. However, of course, not all deaths on the rail track are intentional.

One of the worst incidents happened at Holgate Bridge not very far outside York Station when, on a very foggy day, the train guard jumped off his train into the path of another train and was killed instantly. We were called there to remove the man to hospital for the Coroner's post-mortem examination. The next day in the same fog one of the railway accident investigators was also struck by a train, so in the space of twenty-four hours we were removing another victim.

One Sunday morning I was called to the main London–Scotland railway line near Riccall, about seven miles south of York. Although I was told that there were several police officers there, I did not know how near I could get a vehicle to the scene of the recovery so I called for Harry Cook and he went with me. And it was a good job I did because the place we wanted to be was fairly remote. From the main A19 York–Selby road we turned off into a narrow country lane which eventually turned into a grass track, then over a farm bridge, down another turning into a mud track which terminated at the rail track side. I reckon we had travelled about three miles. At that time there was I think four railway tracks and it was an extremely busy line.

The police officer at the track side told us all trains had been stopped until 12 noon. I looked at my watch and it was 11.40 a.m. I asked how far it was to the scene. He thought about five hundred yards but he was not sure as he had not been there. He also informed us that one of his colleagues was at the scene. In those days we still had not progressed to stretchers, so Harry and I unloaded the removal coffin shell from the hearse, slid it down the grass bank on to the rail track and commenced our walk to the scene. Very soon a dark spot came into view down the track as we came close we realised it was a police officer literally standing guard over the victim. He looked thoroughly miserable and was clearly relieved to see us. The victim was a young man late teens early twenties and had been quite severely mutilated.

We were just about to lift him into the removal shell when a police officer on the bridge further down the track shouted to us with the aid of a megaphone to stop. He added that a pathologist wanted to see the body first. We were fast running out of time for the trains to re-start so we did not think this was a good idea, although I presumed that they would know we were still on the line. Within five minutes the police officer was on his megaphone again informing us that the pathologist had changed his mind and we could proceed. We quickly lifted the body into the removal shell and started our journey down the track. By this time everyone seemed to have disappeared.

After we had gone about fifty yards Harry said, 'You watch the front, I'll watch behind and if you hear a train drop this and head for the side of the track.' We managed to reach the hearse by 12.10 p.m. with no sign of any train. We lifted the coffin shell into the hearse and returned to the old County Hospital at York where the post-mortem was to take place. It transpired, however, that this was not a suicide, nor indeed a straightforward accident. The young man had been a passenger on a football special, I think from Scotland, and somehow had fallen from the train. As he fell it seemed likely that he had been struck by another train. Not far from the scene the police discovered a sheath knife, very probably from the train, which added to the mystery. A few years later the pathologist who carried out the post-mortem gave a talk to our Association (The National Association of Funeral Directors). After the talk I mentioned the incident to him. He remembered it quite clearly and indeed confirmed that the death was suspicious.

Over the years there were some tragic and quite unusual deaths where the circumstances were very unlikely to recur. Having said that, I removed two men within a period of two years who each died on their honeymoon and another young man who died with his girlfriend in the countryside. I never removed ladies who had died in similar circumstances.

Early one morning I was called to a bakery in York where there had been an explosion. The baker had been killed instantly. On another occasion I attended at an accident on a road just outside the city where road repairs were taking place. A workman had died after being involved in an accident with a road roller.

One day I was called to Rowntree's, our well-known confectionery factory in York. A male employee had collapsed and died there. When I arrived, the Coroner's Officer said. 'I hope this gentleman is not a relation of yours. He has the same surname.'

When I arrived at the scene it was indeed a relation. It was my father's cousin, Edwin.

Since I was working for the East Riding Coroner as well I removed people whose deaths had been reported to the Coroner who had died at Fulford Hospital and the psychiatric hospital at Naburn, just outside the city boundary. One Sunday morning I was asked to remove a person from Naburn Hospital to the County Hospital for a post-mortem: not an unusual request. As I arrived at the hospital I started to drive down the road to the mortuary. I was nearly there when I saw a policeman waving at me. I stopped and he quickly informed me that my removal was not from the mortuary but from the hospital grounds. It transpired that a male patient had climbed the hospital clock tower and, once there, had either fallen or taken his own life.

I was called to a lay-by just north of York one morning where a heavy lorry had parked. Another lorry driver had stopped there and had become suspicious and informed the police. Inside they found the young driver. He had been there for quite some time. Whether he had felt ill or had just stopped for a sleep, I do not think anyone was sure; but he had climbed into his bunk bed behind the driving seat, covered himself up, gone to sleep and died.

Sometimes people die or take their own life, and because of certain circumstances or the locality of the death, can remain undiscovered for quite a considerable time. Two such instances always remain clear in my mind. The first one concerned an old gentleman who lived alone in a first floor council flat in York. People occupied the ground floor flat and the flats to either side, yet when the flat was eventually broken into it was discovered that he had been dead for six months. If I recall correctly the inquest had recorded that he had no family and was a loner. Yet there must have been bills and council rent that was unpaid; it always seems very sad when someone can die and not be missed by anyone. But regrettably it has happened before and will surely happen again.

The other instance had an identical time factor but totally different circumstances. I was called late one night to a field about four miles to the south of York where a badly decomposed body had been discovered by a farmer in a field about a quarter of a mile from the roadside. Finding such a location during the day can sometimes be difficult but at night-time it is nearly impossible unless someone can wait on the main road to direct you to the scene. I mentioned this to the police officer. He said there would be no difficulty on this occasion as it was viewed as a suspicious death. There was a pathologist in attendance and the scene was illuminated with arc lamps.

I called for Harry – luckily he had not gone to bed – and we set off. We drove through York and then out into the countryside. True to the police officer's word, as we approached the scene a bright glow appeared in a field to the right. There was a narrow dirt track which I started to drive down. I was able to get to within fifty yards of the scene and we had to walk the rest.

Because of the severe decomposition of the body we had great difficulty with the removal. When we arrived back at York County Hospital the pathologist was ready to start an immediate post-mortem. It transpired when the person had been identified that it was a psychiatric patient who had walked out of the hospital, then walked about two miles down the road into a field, lain down and taken an overdose and died. It was nearly six months later before the farmer discovered the body that night.

I was called, one morning, to The Station Hotel, as it was then known, one of York's largest hotels. I was asked to meet the Coroner's Officer at the rear of the hotel in Station Square where the goods entrance is. Also present were officers of the British Transport Police, whose jurisdiction the hotel then fell under. A coach party of people who were touring the country had an overnight stop in York and next morning were waiting to board the coach to continue their journey. The coach was there but no driver. It was at first thought the driver had probably slept in. I do not think there was a telephone in his room and no response could be got from knocking on his door.

Eventually the hotel staff let themselves into the room and discovered that the poor chap had died in his sleep. There was, however, quite a problem for us. The driver had died in a very small room at the very top of the hotel and somehow we had to get him from there down through the hotel and to the rear entrance in Station Square. Of course the hotel manager was extremely concerned that the hotel guests remained unaware of the driver's unfortunate demise. We had just recently bought our first covered stretcher. It was not as conspicuous as a coffin removal shell and therefore was ideal for such a public place as a hotel.

With the help of the hotel staff standing on guard at corridor ends, we were able to make our way to the hotel lift, but not the guests' lift. This was a service lift which operated at the rear of the hotel and as I understood was mainly used for transporting goods to different floors. It was decided that the stretcher could be propped up against one side of the lift, there being not enough space to lay it down. That left room for one other person, as of course the stretcher had to be accompanied, and that was me. My colleagues said they would meet me down below. They closed the lift gate and pressed the down button, which was outside the lift.

There were no controls inside and consequently I had no power over the descent. It was like travelling in a dumb waiter – very slow and pitch-black, certainly not the best way to travel; but worse was to come. All of a sudden the lift started to shake and then it stopped. There was not a sound. I tried to look up through the lift gate but could see nothing and when I looked down I could just see a chink of light a long way below me. I expected the lift to start almost straight away, but there was not a movement nor a sound. After about five minutes, which seemed considerably longer, I thought I had better do something, so I shouted out but no response. I thought the lift had broken or maybe there had been a power cut. All I could do was sit tight, but in complete darkness that is not easy. Then after what seemed a very long time the lift started to descend and I heard myself saying, 'Please don't stop again!'

Gradually the lift shaft became brighter and then the lift reached the bottom, which appeared to be in a large storeroom. My colleagues thought it was fairly amusing, making cracks like, 'Where have you been?'

I never discovered how the lift came to a halt, but the biggest problem had been that my colleagues could not locate where the lift descended to and I must admit it was fairly well concealed. As far as I am aware up until that day I did not suffer from claustrophobia, but ever since that day I have not cared for travelling in lifts. When I stop at a hotel and it has stairs which will take me to my room, I use them – which keeps me fairly fit as well.

A few years ago we had a holiday in Mexico, ending with ten days in Acapulco. Every night about 8 p.m. there was a complete power cut, not only the hotel but all the streets as well. For what reason I do not know it only lasted about twenty seconds; but if I had been in a lift and it had stopped and then no lights as well I am not sure how I could have handled it. So no lifts for me in Acapulco.

One afternoon I received a telephone call from Gerry Corker, the then Coroner's Officer. He asked me if I could meet Paul Canning, the Deputy Coroner's Officer, at the south door of York Minster. Someone had collapsed and died while visiting the cathedral. It was a very hot and humid day. I drove on my own to the Minster, parked the hearse outside, went inside the south door and found Paul.

I asked him where we were going.

'Hasn't Gerry told you?' he asked.

I replied, 'No, only to meet you here.'

'He's up there,' Paul indicated, pointing up towards the main tower.

For anyone who does not know York Minster, there is a spiral stone staircase just to the left of the south door leading to the top of the cathedral which visitors can use. It is well worth the long climb because there is an excellent view of our beautiful city and the surrounding area from there. I am not sure if this gentleman had been to the top and seen the view or had died on the way up. The remainder of the visitors had been brought out of the tower and now it was Paul's job and mine to remove the unfortunate gentleman. This removal was again done before we had a stretcher, so we were using our coffin removal shell. Paul and I started to climb the staircase. Even with the shell empty we had to have quite frequent rests. The only good thing about it was the gentleman was only about three-quarters of the way up the tower and not at the very top.

We eventually arrived at the scene. It was obvious straight away that he was a big man, which was not going to make our job any easier. Our first problem was actually setting the coffin down on the spiral steps, which had quite an acute angle, and instead of just being able to lay the coffin on a flat surface we had to wedge it from wall to wall across the steps. We managed to lift the gentleman into the shell, which was not easy, and then commenced our descent.

Although going down is obviously far easier than going up, it was a tremendous struggle because even if there had been more of us, it would have been impossible to get more than two of us round the removal shell owing to the narrowness of the staircase. So we went down one at the head and one at the foot, with the man at the foot going backwards. The only thing was, if there had been two more men we could have taken turns which would have given us a rest. After stopping numerous times for rests we eventually reached the bottom, and by this time Paul and I were completely wet through with perspiration. We carried the shell into the hearse through the south door and made our way to the County Hospital where the post-mortem was to take place. Gerry Corker, the Coroner's Officer, apologised for not being there to assist us. Paul and I always thought that there was a certain lack of sincerity in that statement.

I was just leaving the office one Saturday morning when the telephone rang. It was the East Riding police. I was asked to report to a track off the main road leading down to the river to the South of York. Harry had not left so he went with me. I was fairly sure I knew this track and it did not take us long to find a police officer waiting at the roadside. We drove down the track and came to what I can only describe as a stone built outhouse. Inside a man was sat on a chair and in front of him was another chair and on that was tied a double-barrelled shotgun.

I will not go into detail, but he had managed with what I thought was great ingenuity to discharge the weapon. Of course the man had sustained terrible wounds to his head. The only reason this impact had not knocked him over was because the blast had been completely to his head. To get close to the man we started to move the chair on which the shotgun rested. With a voice that made me jump the police officer shouted a warning and moved forward. We stood back and the police officer started to examine the gun. He very gently uncocked the remaining barrel. He had noticed that only one had been discharged and he then untied the gun from the chair. If he had not been so alert maybe there would have been two removals that day. I never ever forgot that incident and with any subsequent instance that involved firearms I knew what to look for.

The Coroner's Officer telephoned me one day and said there had been a road accident in the centre of York. The accident victim had been pronounced dead at the scene and would I attend. It is more usual that road accident victims are removed by ambulance and pronounced dead at the hospital. But on this occasion a doctor had been one of the first people on the scene and pronounced death. At that time we had still not progressed to removal stretchers and the only means of removal we had was a hearse and coffin removal shell. That method was not too bad if you were in a secluded place but in a busy York street it would, in my view, have looked macabre and probably caused more distress to onlookers than was necessary. So I respectfully declined and the removal was carried out with, I think, a police vehicle.

Some days later my father and I discussed the incident and decided we needed an alternative vehicle for such occasions. We discovered a Birmingham coachbuilder who specialised in building hearses and limousines and had developed a purpose-built removal van on a mini chassis. We obtained photographs and specifications and decided that the vehicle was ideal for us and we ordered one straight away. When we took delivery it gave a new dimension to our business.

Just prior to us getting the van we were removing a person who had died at the Military Hospital in York. When we returned to our premises there had been a telephone call from the hospital from the person in charge, a new appointment, I think, complaining because a hearse had driven into the hospital in full view of the wards. This was something we had always done, and some funeral directors still remove from hospitals with a hearse. I personally prefer to be more discreet. By this time we also had the hospital removal contract. This was to convey people who had died in hospitals that came under York Hospital Management to the County Hospital for post-mortem. With the Coroner's work, this became nearly a full-time job for me.

The business was increasing its funeral numbers every year to such an extent that in 1971 we decided to relinquish both the Coroner's and Hospital Management removal contracts so that we could concentrate exclusively on our own funerals. I had learnt a lot in the twelve years we were involved and the experience proved invaluable to me.

Chapter Seven

In 1961 my father decided to take a holiday. That might not sound particularly unusual, but for Father it was. My father and mother were married in August, 1939, had a brief honeymoon at Scarborough, and had never had a holiday together since. I was just short of my twenty-first birthday, so I think my father thought he could take a risk and leave me in charge for a week. To say I was apprehensive does not really describe how I felt. It was something much worse, for this meant that not only would I be responsible for making the coffins, having the vehicles ready and the men to drive them; I would have to arrange and conduct the funerals as well. Other than being involved in the early stages of funeral arrangements, for instance, taking a few details from the family if they called at the office unannounced, I had not arranged and conducted a funeral throughout. The first thing my father did was dispatch me to Len Neale the tailor whose shop was then in Tower Street. My father wanted me to have the full regalia – a frock coat, pinstripes and black topper. As much as I usually did all my father asked me, I point-blank refused the frock coat and topper. I ended up being measured for pinstripes, black jacket and waistcoat and subsequently never wore anything else when conducting a funeral.

My mother and father's holiday was to be taken in our caravan which my father had built himself in 1950, with help from one or two friends and others. It was permanently situated at Ravenscar, a small village on the east coast ten miles north of Scarborough. My mother, my sister, Christine, and myself had spent many holidays there and had great affection for Ravenscar. My father's visits were much more infrequent because of demands from the business and very rarely was he able to stay overnight.

I expect, to be honest, as time was nearing for their holiday departure I was hoping something would turn up to stop them going; not very nice, I must admit, but the thought of running the business for a week on my own made me quite miserable. My father had sensibly taken out some insurance in the shape of Henry Cross, a friend of his who was a funeral director in Moss Street, York, and whose business premises used to be situated in The Crescent which is behind the Odeon cinema in Blossom Street. My father asked Henry and his wife, Ediss, if they would move down to Penley's Grove Street and take up residence there while they were on holiday – supposedly for Ediss to provide meals and look after the house but also Henry would be on hand if I required any professional advice. In fact, after my mother and father had left for their holiday the first funeral that came in I was asked to visit a house to make the arrangements. Henry offered to accompany me and I gladly accepted. On reflection I think this was possibly planned by Henry and my father.

I discovered in later years in conversation with other funeral directors that arranging the first funeral is quite a milestone and once it is over one's confidence starts to build up. That was certainly the case with me and after that first funeral I made the arrangements on my own. That did not mean that I did not need help and advice; I did, but after that first experience it was more a matter of getting confirmation that the arrangements I had made were correct and that nothing had been left out.

After my father, Henry Cross was a great help to me in the following years. If my father was not there I could always telephone or go and see Henry if I needed advice. It's funny how things in life come round to where you start, and now one or two young funeral directors telephone me very often at home to ask my advice. Although extremely competent and fairly well experienced, they too, like myself all those years before, sometimes need confirmation or assurance on certain aspects or situations in their business.

I managed to get through that first week and was never as nervous again, but I was always a little apprehensive whenever father decided he would have a holiday.

The following year I married Elaine, who lived at Cawood, a village ten miles south of York. Her mother's sister, Rusty, was married to Raymond Garbutt who was in business in Cawood with his father as joiners, builders and funeral directors. After our marriage we spent quite a lot of our time on evenings out with Raymond and Rusty, and Raymond and I became great friends. Unfortunately Rusty died in 1969, but Raymond and I still have a drink together most weekends and of course we both had something else in common – the funeral profession.

We were now getting extremely short of space at St Andrewgate and the old building was becoming very shabby outside and in. Although the garage accommodation for the fleet had been relieved considerably by us leasing The Bay Horse Hotel garage at Monk Bar, about five minutes walk from our premises. My father and I had been nattering at Harry Atha, the licensee, for quite some time to see if he would consider leasing the hotel's garage to us. The Atha family had been licensees at The Bay Horse for many years and our families knew each other quite well. Gillian, Harry's younger daughter, and myself were at school together. Margaret, Gillian's sister, and her husband printed stationery for our firm and David, their brother, was the licensee for many years. At that time we were desperately short of space for our fleet, which we wanted to increase, and my father and myself always felt we owed a debt of gratitude to Harry and his wife, Nellie, for helping us at that time.

Of course, it was not just garage space we were short of. We only had one office and in that office families arranged funerals, waited there to be shown into the Chapel and paid accounts. Naturally, that is where most of the administration was carried out. The only form of heating we had was a paraffin stove. We decided we would convert what was the Chapel of Rest into an additional office and erect a building in what was the garden, which was in between the house and the workshop. We also applied for planning permission to demolish the whole building and reconstruct, but this was rejected. The main reason was the York City Council wanted businesses out of that area so it could conform to Lord Esher's Plan which was to return the area just within the City walls to residential dwellings as it had been many years before. My father and I were certainly not in sympathy with that idea at the time, but I must confess now that the Esher Plan certainly compliments the Old City. Unhappily there are other developments in the Old City which, in my view, do not.

Before we could put our alterations into practice, the house next door to where my father lived in Penley's Grove Street came on the market. It was the home of Mr and Mrs Bill Granger and family.

Very similar to my father's house, it was a double fronted detached Georgian house with spacious rooms. It had a large garden to the rear and beyond that a yard with several simple garages which Mr Granger rented out. In between Mr Granger's house and my father's was a lane which gave access to the garages, one of which my father rented. My father's first suggestion was that we try to purchase the land at the rear, demolish the garages and build one large garage for the fleet. I suggested – and it must have been one of my first useful ideas – that we purchase the house as well and hopefully get planning permission to change from residential to commercial use, sell St Andrewgate and move the business lock, stock and barrel to Penley's Grove Street.

The first problem, could we afford it? How much could we sell St Andrewgate for? What would we require to borrow to demolish the old garages and then erect a large new one? Well, we managed to overcome the financial side and the change of use and we bought the property; but the thing that really worried my father was the actual moving of the business. After all, we had been at St Andrewgate since 1848 and many of the families just turned up when they wanted us. My father had visions of families coming to St Andrewgate, not finding us there and going elsewhere for the funeral. However, by now increasing numbers of families had telephones and phoned us first before coming to the office. We of course also decided to publicise our move with notices in the *Yorkshire Evening Press*, York's local newspaper.

Shortly before we moved the *Yorkshire Evening Press* contacted my father and asked if they could come down to St Andrewgate and interview him about the move and also get a story in relation to the history of the business. The article appeared in the *Press* alongside a photograph of my father outside the office at St Andrewgate. This of course helped to publicise our move and at the same time hopefully provided an interesting story for the readers. Needless to say, we were always extremely grateful to the *Yorkshire Evening Press* for this unsolicited help at this very important time.

We sold our premises at St Andrewgate to a local bakery firm and in due course picked a day for our removal – not any ordinary move after being in business in premises for one hundred and nineteen years. The one place of work that was smaller at Penley's Grove Street was the workshop; where we had four workbenches at St Andrewgate our new workshop could only accommodate two. But we had ample storerooms, a large garage which could hold twelve limousines and hearses if required, and the luxury of more than adequate office space. There were two offices to begin with, a reception and waiting room combined and my father's office for interviews on the ground floor. In later years we developed two more offices on the first floor: an accounts office and a further interviewing office. We also had a Chapel and preparation room at the rear on the ground floor. Achieving all this without any structural alterations was an added bonus for us.

There had been one or two objections from residents who did not like the idea of a funeral director on the doorstep but these were rejected by the Council. In my view, people's concern are perfectly understandable. They have visions of coffins going in and out of the building at regular intervals. But there have to be funeral directors; just like crematoriums and cemeteries, they are a fact of life and have to go somewhere. and they are not much use miles away from the population. I think, however, it is the duty of a funeral director who opens new premises to be discrete and camouflage his activities as best he can. The one stipulation imposed on us by the Council was that coffins must not go in and out of the front door. That was never our intention so it was not a problem.

One of the first things we realised very quickly was that we were not going to be able to leave our new premises unmanned as we had done at St Andrewgate. Bert Smith, who had worked part-time in the office at St Andrewgate, was then about eighty. He was very fit and active but it was quite obvious we now needed a full-time receptionist and secretary and within a month J. Rymer had engaged their first lady employee. The transformation was incredible. All of a sudden we had moved from working in what had become run-down premises into near luxury premises in comparison. It gave both my father and me a lift. At St Andrewgate we had sometimes felt like having to apologise for the poor old office, especially in winter with the paraffin stove.

Soon after we moved to Penley's Grove Street, John Fry died. John was the proprietor of James Walker and Sons, Carriage Masters, of Clarence Street, York. They supplied hearses and limousines to some of the smaller funeral directors, primarily those whose main profession was something else like builders or joiners, whom I have referred to earlier. Up to that time we were supplying about twelve funeral directors and James Walker about the same number. My father and I decided fairly quickly that we must acquire the business if at all possible. This we managed to do. Fortunately we did not have to buy the property, just the goodwill and the fleet, which consisted of a Humber Snipe low line hearse and I think four Humber Pullman limousines. Of course we had plenty of room for these in our new garage.

We now had three hearses and six limousines. This was as large as our fleet ever got, even though our own business was still on the increase. A combination of two things ensured that the fleet would only get smaller in the following years. Firstly, there were more families owning their own cars and using them to attend funerals; secondly the gradual disappearance of some of the smaller funeral directors, due mainly to their arriving at retiring age and not having anyone to follow them on, a circumstance compounded by some having a son who was reluctant to be a funeral director.

The Humber Snipe hearse we acquired when we bought James Walker did not last long. Henry Cross and I went to Leeds to remove someone from a hospital. On our return we had a puncture on the outskirts of Leeds. Not having the vehicle very long I did not know where the jack and spare wheel where. I eventually discovered a compartment built into the deck of the hearse. The problem was the coffin, which was laid on top of the hatch, and although the coffin would move a little way to the side it was not enough to be able to open it. The only possible way to get at the spare wheel was to remove the coffin completely from the vehicle. Henry and I soon decided this was not an option. If we removed the coffin the only place to put it would be on the road. Pedestrians and motorists would wonder what the devil was going on; plus it was the kind of incident, that could quite possibly attract a photographer. Henry and I decided to telephone the office and seek guidance. Fortunately there was a telephone box quite near. Father decided to send out one of the other hearses to us, transfer the coffin quickly then change the wheel. We very quickly decided that this hearse had to go, but before we changed it I had to take a coffin from Heathrow Airport to York. Before I set off I removed the spare wheel from the compartment and stood it inside the hearse; better safe than sorry.

Round about this time I met Rod Milne for the first time. He was the senior partner at Coleman Milne Coachbuilders of Bolton in Lancashire. I am not absolutely sure, but I think they were the first firm in this country to buy ordinary standard production line saloon cars – in the early days these were all Fords – cut them in two, lengthen the chassis and then build it back together with a glass division to separate the driver from the passengers. They then put in an extra row of seats and made a limousine that would seat six people in the rear compartment, popularly known as a 'stretched limousine'. It was far more economical to produce limousines in this way by using production line models than to use purpose-built limousines such as

Daimlers or Rolls-Royce. Rod came to York to see us for the first time I think late in 1968 or early 1969. Before he left we had ordered our first Ford Diplomat limousine from him. The name was later changed to Dorchester, as they discovered that there was already I believe a French car with the same name.

Before we took delivery of our new vehicle we accepted an order for three or maybe four days' chauffeur drive to tour York and the surrounding area. There was just one passenger – Mrs Charlton Heston. Our Humber Pullman limousines, although still tidy, were getting a bit long in the tooth. I telephoned Rod but there was no chance of our vehicle being ready in time. I then told him who our client was and he kindly offered to lend us his demonstrator limousine. Mrs Heston enjoyed her stay in York and wrote us a very nice letter thanking us. She also said she would bring her husband to York hopefully some time in the future. Well, eventually he did come to York, twenty years later. He was appearing at the York Theatre Royal in a play on a pre-West End run, and we provided a limousine for his use while he was here, conveying him to and from his hotel to the theatre.

In subsequent years we not only bought limousines off Coleman Milne but hearses too, and by the mid-1970s our fleet was completely supplied by them. Coleman Milne was a tremendous success; they expanded very rapidly, had a large stand at the Motor Show each year and exported their vehicles worldwide. They went on to improvise by converting many other makes of vehicle. Rod sold out in the early 1980s and sadly died soon after. Later, Coleman Milne merged with Woodall Nicholson Coachbuilders of Halifax, whom we had previously bought hearses from. They are still to this day producing hearses and limousines for our profession from their new factory at West Houghton near Wigan.

Chapter Eight

In 1972 the National Association of Funeral Directors decided to arrange a professional tour of the United States of America. My father, who had been to the USA in 1964 with my mother, said I should go. It did not take a great deal of thought from me to think this was a good idea; to see the American funeral profession at close hand would be interesting, but more of an attraction for me was to see the USA for the first time. I asked Ray Garbutt if he would accompany me and he agreed. The Association arranged for us to visit funeral homes, as they are referred to there, in New York, San Francisco, Los Angeles and Miami. The original party consisted of about sixty people. Some were husbands and wives, some were business colleagues like Raymond and myself and a few were travelling on their own. The tour was arranged for October of that year and would last two weeks. However, in June a BEA Trident airliner crashed at Staines shortly after taking off from Heathrow, and all 118 passengers and crew died. This had the effect of making several of the party cancel, which reduced our numbers to somewhere between forty and fifty.

After we arrived in New York our first visit was to Campbell's Funeral Home, an opulent building. When we got inside it reminded me of an hotel. It was indeed a complete funeral home; everything was done there on the premises, from arranging funerals and post-mortems to embalming and cosmetics. There was also a showroom with about fifty caskets, from which families could select, and a large chapel for funeral services catering for all denominations. There were three or four floors with several suites on each floor; the suites varied in size, some having two, three or four rooms. In the main room, which was furnished like a lounge, lay the casket with the deceased; doors led of this main room to a bedroom and bathroom, and with some larger suites additional rooms. The idea was that if the family so wished they could spend the days leading up to the funeral with their relative. I was told Campbell's would probably arrange and conduct about one thousand funerals per year.

Also in New York, but by way of a complete contrast, we visited the funeral directors Hess-Miller Inc. About the only thing they had in common with Campbell's was their sheer professionalism. Their premises consisted of a one-storey building with office, chapel and four rest rooms. They hired in their hearses and limousines from a larger funeral director who also carried out their removals. They did not keep anything on the premises whatsoever and would take the family to a manufacturer's showroom to select the casket. They probably arranged and conducted about one hundred funerals per annum and managed to make a comfortable living without an additional occupation.

That was 1972, and no funeral director in this country would have been able to make his sole income from one hundred funerals; and I am not aware of one today who could do so. Obviously their profit margin in the USA was higher but in contrast the majority of British funeral directors have always been apprehensive about appearing to charge too much. In my view, the vast majority of British funeral directors give an excellent professional service, but very often their charges fail to reflect the service they provide.

From New York we flew to San Francisco – just as long a flight as from London to New York. We were allowed access to the top deck of the American Airlines 747. When we got up there we found a lounge bar with tables not unlike any American lounge bar on the ground, and set right in the middle was an electric organ. Quite a few of our NAFD colleagues were already there being served with drinks by air stewardesses, as they were still called then, doubling as barmaids. I played a few tunes on the organ and those of us who were there had a few drinks. It was quite the most relaxing and enjoyable flight I have ever had. Shortly before we touched down at San Francisco, the bar staff informed us that they had completely run out of alcohol, the first time this had ever happened. Obviously their stock must have been quite low when we left New York. As we disembarked the pilot was descending the staircase from the top deck. He obviously knew who we were and said he wished to take a look at us because this was the first time anyone had ever drunk one of his planes dry!

San Francisco, as I think anyone knows who has visited it, is quite different from nearly anywhere else in the USA and in 1972 people from our country had not yet started visiting it in any great numbers. As well as our professional appointments we went to the usual tourist sites such as Alcatraz, Muir Woods to see the giant Redwoods, China-town, the Golden Gate Bridge, and of course we rode on the famous cable cars.

The most interesting and informative place we visited professionally was a casket manufacturer called California Caskets. Here, men made the caskets and women made the linings and interiors and fitted them. The casket had sprung mattresses which could be raised or lowered to whatever height was required. We had nothing like this back home. In addition there was a large showroom with about sixty caskets for families to select from. The larger funeral directors would have their own showrooms, but as in New York with Hess-Miller Inc., this showroom was available to the smaller funeral directors.

We also should have visited another casket manufacturer who traded under the wonderful name of Golden Gate Caskets but regrettably they went into liquidation shortly before our arrival in San Francisco; or did they know we were coming?

There was just one unpleasant incident while we were in San Francisco. One morning two of our colleagues woke to discover that whilst they had slept their hotel room had been broken into and ransacked. How they had managed to sleep through it I do not know. The police of course were called by the hotel management and during their interview the two victims had remarked that they wished they had been woken up by the thieves. The policemen said they were lucky not to have been awoken. They would have very likely lost more than their belongings.

On our last night in San Francisco, Raymond and I were in the hotel bar – where else! Later on in the evening a group of performers from a show at a nearby theatre came into the bar. One of them got on the piano and the others sang songs for about an hour. We were lucky to have been there that night as it was a very enjoyable way to end our visit to San Francisco. Next stop, Los Angeles.

Of our visits here the most outstanding was to Forest Lawns Memorial Park at Glendale. This is one of the four cemeteries which belong to Forest Lawns in Los Angeles, the others being at Hollywood Hills, Covina Hills and Cypress. They were established in 1917 by Dr Hubert Eaton and became known as the Memorial Park Plan. Of the many innovations he introduced one was of placing memorial stones flush with the lawn in place of the conventional method of vertical memorials. Instead of headstones at Forest Lawns they became memorial tablets. Trees were planted, vast sweeping lawns laid out, ponds created for ducks and swans, with fountains and statues; but for me the most impressive things at Forest Lawns are its churches, all built as replicas of other churches, some in the USA the others from Britain.

The American churches include the Church of the Hills, a replica of the old New England Meeting House in which the Poet Henry Wordsworth Longfellow worshipped; then Boston's Old North Church, closely associated with Paul Revere. The British Churches are the Little Church of Flowers, inspired by the church at Stoke Poges where Thomas Gray wrote his Elegy. Then there is the Church of the Recessional, a reproduction of St Margaret in Rottingdean at which Rudyard Kipling worshipped; and finally a church from Scotland, the Wee Kirk O' The Heather, a replica of the kirk in Glencairn where Annie Laurie worshipped. The pulpit in this church was made in Scotland. All the churches are inter-denominational and in addition to funeral services many marriages and baptisms take place here.

One statistic I remember from the time I was there is that Forest Lawn employed around ninety representatives who were engaged in selling plots of land around the clock.

Forest Lawn, as you might have guessed, are funeral directors as well, so if you wished they did the lot, but with absolute professionalism and dignity.

Before we left Los Angeles four of us hired a car and drove to Long Beach on our free day. We had dinner on the *Queen Mary* and I played my first game of pool in a local bar.

Our final stop was Miami, our flight arriving late in the evening. After dinner at our hotel Raymond and I had a good walk. For both of us it was our first experience of a really hot climate. We ended the night in a bar opposite the hotel and I regret to say we did not leave until 5 a.m. As a result, we missed our visit the next morning in Miami. They have a crematorium there which uses the calcination process involving immediate disintegration. I do not appear to have any data on this process but as far as I am aware we do not have anything like it here in this country.

Our tour ended with a cocktail party in Mr and Mrs Gerry Carter's penthouse suite. Gerry was our national president and had led our visit to the USA. I think the tour was an outstanding success, we made a lot of contacts and friends and it was the forerunner of many subsequent NAFD tours. I like the USA and the people and have visited several times since.

Chapter Nine

Around about this time we started to have our first contact with deaconesses. At first it seemed unusual for a lady to be conducting a funeral service. One day Keith, our senior funeral director, returned to the office after making funeral arrangements and came into my office. All had gone well until he mentioned to the lady whose husband had died that there was a possibility that a lady might conduct the service. She immediately stated that under no circumstances was a lady going to conduct her husband's funeral service. Fortunately the procedure at the church where the service was to take place was that we contacted the rector first. This Keith did and the rector literally went up the wall when Keith passed on the lady's comments. Keith terminated the telephone conversation fairly quickly and informed me. I then telephoned the rector and tried to sort out the problem.

The gist of it was that he was not going to be told who could or could not conduct services in his church, and of course he was right. I explained that all we were doing was conveying the wishes of the family to him and if we did not do that we were not doing our job, which is to arrange a funeral as close to a family's wishes as possible. He then realised the position we were in and said he would visit the family himself. I do not know what happened at that visit but the rector ended up conducting the service himself.

Of course it is not unusual now for ladies to conduct services, and I cannot recall any more objections since that original occurrence. My father had said to me very early on in my career that you must respect every one's religion. During the course of our work we come into contact with nearly every religion, although in the York area the vast majority of the funeral services are Church of England, Roman Catholic or the Free Church (Methodist). But we also have funeral services from the minority religions and we must have knowledge of their procedures with regard to the funeral service. I do not think anyone would expect a funeral director to have expert and first-hand knowledge of all these minority religions, so the National Association of Funeral Directors provides its members with a reference section in its manual which deals explicitly with minority religions, their customs and procedures. However, the same criterion applies as with all funerals; the family's wishes are paramount.

Of course, there are also non-religious services; these usually fall into the category of humanist or secular services, where during the course of the service or gathering one or more of the family or friends will recall that person's life and achievements.

At an atheist funeral there can very often be nothing at all, whether it is cremation or interment. If cremation is chosen, the coffin must go via the crematorium chapel to the crematorium. It will depend on the instructions of the person who has died whether anyone accompanies the coffin to the chapel or not. I have seen both. If the funeral is to be interment, the hearse will go direct to the cemetery, again, accompanied or not depending on the deceased's instructions. The coffin is removed from the hearse, carried to the grave and lowered in; it is very final without some words of comfort. The person who has died is an atheist, but their family may not be, and it can be distressing for them. Nevertheless, at the end of the day, it is the family, and funeral director's duty to carry out the deceased's final instructions.

Funeral services can be traumatic so I expect it is not surprising that some ministers and in some cases families try to lessen the stress by moving away from the conventional form of funeral service. The most common form of service is, for a cremation, a service at church followed by a committal service at the crematorium chapel, or alternatively the full service at the crematorium leaving out the church. If the funeral is to be interment there is a service at church followed by the committal service at the graveside. If the cemetery has a chapel the service could take place there rather than the church and sometimes, but not very often, there is just a graveside service not preceded by a service elsewhere.

Let us now look at some of the alternative funeral services. Firstly there is the private funeral, which can take the form of a service where only the immediate members of the family will attend. The deceased may have left instructions for such a service to take place, or the family may make the decision themselves. I think probably the advantage of this form of service to some people would be the absence of a large congregation, which some families can find overwhelming. There is the private funeral service followed at a later date by a memorial service, and this is much favoured by politicians and show business personalities. Some families decide to have the funeral service and committal service all at church. Then the coffin will proceed either to the crematorium or cemetery on its own.

I have known this choice being made but it has then been decided that at least one member of the family would escort the coffin to the crematorium or cemetery. As two sons once said to me, 'We don't want Dad going on his own.' They followed the hearse to the crematorium, walked behind the coffin into the chapel, remained there for two or three minutes and then left to rejoin their mother and the rest of the family.

A few years ago I was asked to arrange a funeral in a way that I had never encountered before, although I am quite sure my colleagues elsewhere had; it has happened once or twice since but is relatively uncommon in our area. I was instructed to arrange a time at the crematorium for a short service and committal and then to arrange a service at their church to follow on immediately; so on the day we went in cortège from the family home to the crematorium, carried the coffin into the chapel, had the short service and then the cremation took place. I then escorted the family to the limousines (of course, we did not require the hearse) then proceeded to the church for what had now become a memorial service. The obituary notice had not given any indication that the service was anything other than a conventional funeral service so I made sure that the minister made an announcement prior to our arrival at church so the congregation understood the absence of the coffin. These are some of the alternative services; there are other variations but I think I have covered the main ones.

Remaining on the subject of letting the congregation know what is going on at a funeral service, regrettably there are sometimes multiple or more likely double funerals, usually the result of an accident, or maybe a husband or wife dying from just plain shock at the loss of a partner. Extra care is required by the funeral director in these circumstances. I will concentrate on double funerals, as multiple funerals – in my own personal experience, I am pleased to say – are rare. Obviously for a family to lose two of its members at the same time is extremely distressing, regardless of the circumstances. If it is husband and wife it is reasonably straightforward; there is only one family to look after. If it is, say, two brothers and one or both are married, or an engaged couple, then you have to deal with two families and then it can become more involved. Obviously both families will have agreed to the double funeral but they might have their own views on what form it should take, so a compromise must be reached. It is quite likely in these circumstances that the funeral director's advice is sought.

The first thing a funeral director realises when arranging his first double funeral is that he needs two of everything: two coffins, two hearses and two sets of documentation. If the service is to take place at church, two sets of trestles will be needed to stand the coffins on. Very soon after the service has commenced, the minister conducting the service must identify whose coffin is which. The only identity the coffins have is the nameplate, which cannot be seen by the congregation, and regardless of the relationship or non-relationship of the deceased, it is quite likely that quite a number of the congregation are really only attending one funeral. An example would be work colleagues of a man who had died but had maybe never met his wife.

Double funeral services can be held at the crematorium or at church, followed by a committal service at a crematorium or cemetery. Recently two brothers died within a few hours of each other. They had both married and it was agreed by both their families that a double service would take place at church; but one family decided on cremation and the other on interment. After the service at church we carried one of the brothers out of church, placed the coffin in one of the hearses and both families followed in cortège to the cemetery. Then we returned to church, carried the other brother from the church, placed him in the second hearse and both families again went in cortège but this time to the crematorium. As far as I am aware the first time for our firm that a double funeral had ended in this way.

Just one final point for a funeral director arranging his first double funeral: before he leaves his premises he will have eight or maybe twelve bearers with him. It is imperative that they know which coffin they are to carry. At a normal single funeral the bearers will know their position to carry, whether at the front of the coffin or the back and if using the left or right shoulder. A double funeral is completely different; there are two hearses and they must have their bearer positions decided before the funeral commences. When the hearses arrive where the service is to take place the limousines are immediately behind the hearses with the family looking in their direction; for them to see the bearers wandering about aimlessly makes the whole thing look amateurish and, of course, less dignified.

One of the things that can concern a funeral director is when there is a request for volunteer bearers. Of course it is the duty of every funeral director to comply with the family's wishes, but carrying a coffin safely, especially a heavy one, requires a certain amount of skill and considerable practice. The volunteers can be sons, grandsons or other family members of the deceased; another example could be a police officer's colleagues, or work colleagues. With all these there is one overwhelming fear for the funeral director – that they drop the coffin. It is less of a concern if the church or chapel where the service is to take place is level but some of the churches have steps, and some are fairly steep. In these circumstances as the coffin is carried up the steps the bearers at the front will drop the coffin down into their hands. The bearers at the rear keep the coffin on their shoulders until they all reach the top of the steps; then the coffin is lifted back on to the front bearers' shoulders. This is no problem for experienced bearers but a real hazard for volunteers.

Over the years we have arranged many travellers' funerals. Sometimes the funeral is arranged at a house but very often it is arranged at a caravan. It is extremely likely that the majority of the family will want the best quality of everything connected with the funeral. They are very likely to want a casket rather than a coffin and will have clear ideas about the casket colour, particularly the interior lining and robe. They will almost certainly have the deceased in the house or caravan on the days leading to the funeral, whether they have died in hospital or at home. The room or caravan will be decorated with drapes and there will be many visitors to view the deceased, especially on the day of the funeral when literally hundreds of fellow travellers will arrive at the home. It would not be an unusual occurrence for us to take the casket into the house or caravan through a window, as some doors are just not wide enough. On occasions we have had to have a glazier in attendance to remove a window when we have taken the casket home, and then again on the day of the funeral.

The very fact that hundreds of people are attending the funeral can also be a problem. They will converge on the house or caravan in their own transport on the day of the funeral, some in cars, some in trucks, which can be used to convey the great number of floral tributes which will arrive at the home. The family may perhaps order six limousines for the immediate family, sometimes supplemented by one or two coaches for those who have no transport or prefer not to follow in their own cars, so the cortège could consist of one or maybe two hearses, the additional hearse solely for the purpose of carrying flowers; maybe six limousines; one or two coaches and numerous private vehicles.

Once a cortège of this size is on the move it is capable of causing disruption to other road users, so it is always advisable to inform traffic control at the local police station about the funeral and intended route for the cortège. The police in turn would advise us if any alteration to that route should be taken for a smoother passage. The funeral will almost certainly finish at a cemetery or burial ground where the grave has probably been lined with flowers. Very few travellers choose cremation. The proceedings culminate with a lavish meal at a hotel, pub, restaurant or club and everyone is invited.

The travellers know what they want, are very unlikely to accept a compromise and are prepared to pay for it. If the funeral director and his staff do the job right they will tell you and be most grateful. They are certainly not reluctant to tell you if there has been something they did not like, and will quite probably ask for the funeral account to reflect any misdemeanour.

Exhumation is something that the funeral director is not involved with all that frequently but I will list the circumstances where it might be required. Very infrequently, and I must emphasise infrequently, thank goodness, someone is interred in a wrong grave or should not have been interred at all. Most hospitals and funeral directors have strict procedures with regard to the identification of bodies. However, sometimes a mistake occurs; the wrong body is removed from the hospital, or on the day of the funeral the wrong body is removed from the funeral director's chapel. If the funeral is at the crematorium and the cremation has taken place before the mistake is discovered, quite obviously nothing can be done; but if the funeral is interment you can exhume. Records at some cemeteries and churchyards are incomplete and quite a number of graves do not have headstones.

This results sometimes regrettably in someone being interred in the wrong grave. The mistake may not be discovered until some member of the family dies who has the burial rights to this grave. The gravedigger attempts to reopen the grave and finds there is no room. There would then have to be an exhumation. Sometimes a burial has taken place and then it is discovered that a valuable piece of jewellery has been buried with the deceased. These circumstances could warrant an exhumation. It has been known for a new road development to cause a mass exhumation so the plans can proceed. Some years ago in one or our local cemeteries several graves of Italian servicemen were exhumed and reinterred in Italy, and from the same cemetery German servicemen were exhumed and reinterred in the German Military Cemetery at Cannock Chase.

HM Coroner has the authority to order an exhumation if he or the police feel an examination of the person interred is desirable. In these cases if an exhumation is required and that person is interred in a cemetery an exhumation order from the Home Office is required. If the interment is in a churchyard a faculty is required and must be obtained through the local Diocesan Registry. If cremated remains are to be exhumed the same procedure must be followed. once a coffin has entered a crematorium, no matter for how short a time, for that coffin to leave the crematorium for whatever reason a Home Office order must be obtained.

Finally before I leave exhumation I must mention an incident which happened not too long ago. We had a funeral service at a village church followed by interment in the churchyard. Several days later a gentleman visiting his wife's grave discovered that it had recently been opened and someone interred; in fact, all the floral tributes were still laid on the grave. The rector was informed and he in turn contacted us to inform us that our interment had taken place in another family's grave.

On this occasion the gravedigger had just reopened the wrong grave. The difference between this exhumation and any other that we have been involved with was that the grave we should have used was next to the one where the interment had taken place, so what we had to do was dig out both graves then just slide the coffin across into the correct grave without lifting the coffin from the grave.

Although technically this was not an exhumation we were moving the coffin from one grave to another and we still required a faculty. As I said earlier, exhumation for the funeral director is not an everyday occurrence but when the circumstances are similar to the one I have just related it can cause great distress to the families involved.

The funeral director's main function at an exhumation is to carry it out with dignity and reverence with the minimum distress to the families. At the same time he must be in full compliance with all conditions imposed by the Home Office and the bishop's faculty, the Environmental Health Officer and the Health and Safety Executive.

Chapter Ten

A few years ago we arranged the funeral of a lady who was a relation of Mr Julian Litten, a curator at The Victoria and Albert Museum; more importantly as far as we were concerned he is a funeral historian and in particular is an authority on English funeral customs. It was a unique experience for us all to make arrangements with someone who knew more about funerals that we did. Of course I cannot go into precise details of the arrangements because of the confidentiality clause in our Code of Practice. Sufficient to say he knew exactly what he wanted and was personally involved in every aspect of the funeral arrangements.

I think it is fair to say that Mr Litten does not approve of the majority of our present day funerals. He regards them as bawdy affairs with criticism of the quality of coffins and a lack of choice – in other words the 'customising' of funerals. The idea of a funeral with no service at church and only a service at a crematorium does not appeal to Mr Litten. He deplores the absence of a cortège, that is when it has been decided that the hearse will proceed on its own to the service and the family travels there independently either in a limousine or in their own cars. He noted that very few families have the coffin home on the night preceding the funeral and that many funeral directors have noticed a decline in the numbers of people visiting the chapel of rest to view the deceased. He goes on to say that mourning dress has virtually disappeared and that staff uniform at some funeral directors has moved from black to either grey or blue. In conclusion he noted that funerals cost less now in relative terms than at any time since the eighteenth century, and thinks it is extraordinary that some people are prepared to spend several thousand pounds on a wedding, yet are reluctant to pay considerably less for a funeral.

Well, I can answer that one for him. A wedding is a joyous occasion when everyone is looking forward to the future, with hopefully many years of happiness ahead; but no one wants a funeral. It is the end of the life, at least as we know it. Very often it is saying goodbye to a much loved father or mother, and you cannot quite obviously expect the same keenness to spend a lot of money. Of course to some extent Mr Litten is correct. A lot of funerals are as he described and he seems to place the main responsibility for that on the trade. All these comments appear in the introduction to Mr Litten's book *The English Way of Death*, published in 1991, and precede his account of the history of funerals in this country since 1450. So let us look at some of his main points of criticism.

Firstly, the coffins. Well, Mr Litten says he has no intention of being sent off in a multi-density fibreboard veneered coffin with plastic handles and terylene lining. A large percentage of coffins used are veneered oak but the majority of funeral directors will have a wider choice of coffins to show their clients, either with a brochure, or a presenter, which not only has photographs but also some detachable samples of the wood used for the coffin, and finally a selection room where the coffins available are displayed. The clients can then if they wish not only inspect the exterior of the coffin but would be able to choose the colour and style of the robe and lining for the interior. Not all funeral directors have selection rooms, but using one of the other methods should be able to give clients a more than satisfactory choice. It must always be remembered by the funeral director that it is not everyone who will be happy to walk round a room full of coffins or even look through a brochure, and if that is the case he must improvise.

I cannot see any criticism of the funeral directors' premises in Mr Litten's book but it is hard to see that a modern funeral directors' premises would meet with his approval. I think that most funeral directors had decided quite some years ago that their premises need not look like what the public would perhaps envisage: a dark painted building with drab curtains on display, the old image thought quite naturally to be in keeping with death and mourning. The consequence of this décor was that families who were already upset had to arrange the funeral in a setting which made them feel worse rather than better. Many of the offices and reception rooms today have delicate pastel shades of wallpaper and curtaining, with carpeting to match, and maybe pine furniture, which completely changes the old image of the funeral directors.

Our premises in York were refurbished recently and we had comments from the public such as, 'It was more like an hotel than a funeral directors'. When a family have to arrange a funeral and decide to do that at the funeral directors' rather than at home they are probably wondering what they are coming to. It is still a difficult job for them to have to do but it must be less of an ordeal for them if they are able to do this in a relaxing environment. Funeral directors' premises vary a great deal in size, design and age. They can be anything from converted houses to purpose-built constructions. We personally consider it extremely important that they are refurbished in a style that is in keeping with each individual building and have a professional interior designer who is responsible for each refurbishment.

Julian Litten is right: funerals have changed, and so have funeral directors; and overall we think the public get the funeral they want. There is absolutely nothing to prevent the public having the kind of funeral Mr Litten prefers, and a minority do; but the fact is the vast majority of families in this country want a quiet, dignified funeral without ostentation. Julian Litten refers to funerals today as something akin to a package holiday. If all funerals were as he preferred they would be more like a luxury cruise with a price to match.

In 1987 Julian Litten was made the first Honorary Member of the British Institute of Funeral Directors in recognition of his research into the history of the trade and indeed his book, *The English Way of Death*, provides an excellent comprehensive reference for anyone, funeral directors or laymen, who are interested in the history of our profession.

In November, 1994, I was invited to be a speaker at a seminar on the National Funeral Project, a group dedicated to restoring the dignity of dying, chaired by the Consumer's Association founder, Lord Young of Dartington. They arranged other seminars in venues throughout the country. Also speaking at the York Seminar were Cannon Terence Grigg, a member of the Consumer Group on Funerals; The Reverend Zuhaii Ahmad, Imam of the Bull Lane Mosque in York; the Reverend Frances Biseker of South York Methodist Circuit; and Jenny Hockey, a University of Hull lecturer and author of a booklet called 'Making the Most of a Funeral'. A further contribution came from Dr Julia Rugg, who is carrying out research at the University of York into burial reform which includes the reuse of burial grounds and cemeteries. This is certainly a controversial subject.

Around about 70 per cent of funerals in Britain are cremations. The majority of the remaining ones are interments; many of the cemeteries in the cities are full, as are the churchyards in rural areas. Some are able to acquire additional land for extensions and some are not. The consequence is that in some areas there is a great shortage of space. Dr Rugg is looking into the possibility of reusing the land after a period of time. I believe seventy-five years was mentioned. Of course, permission would have to be obtained by the families who are in possession of the burial rights of such graves. The National Funeral Project reported their finding in January 1996 in the form of a Death Charter. Some of the criticisms of the funeral profession in the project seem to form a parallel with Julian Litten's comments, such as lack of choice and funerals being rushed. I think I can speak for all the members of our profession in saying that we are never complacent about the standard of funerals we offer and will always be prepared to consider constructive advice and new ideas that anyone might put forward.

When there is an article written or a broadcast about our profession it is inevitable that the cost of funerals will arise, so let us just look now where these costs come from and how a funeral account is made up. Generally speaking a funeral account is in three parts:

1. The funeral director's fees.

2. Statutory or mandatory fees.

3. Optional fees.

Let us look at the funeral director's fees and what he must supply for the funeral:

1. The provision and fitting of a coffin.

2. The removal of the deceased from the place of death. This could be a hospital in another part of the country. Sometimes there are additional journeys required; maybe a removal to the house or a reception into church prior to the service taking place there, often done the evening before.

3. Preparation and care of the deceased until the day of the funeral, having the facilities and staff available for family and friends to visit the chapel of rest if so desired, sometimes out of hours.

4. The provision of hearse and limousine if required on the day of the funeral and a removal vehicle.

5. A 24-hour service. The smallest firm in the country must have a minimum of two persons available at all times. If a person dies in hospital there is no great urgency for a removal, but if the death occurs at home or in a nursing home the removal may be required in a short space of time. We decided at J. Rymer several years ago that the most equitable way was to spread the cost of the 24-hour service among all our clients; after all no one knows whether they are going to die at 3 p.m. or 3 a.m., or where.

6. The costs involved in administration. On top of this are the overhead costs of specialised premises. In use 24 hours a day, they can consist of offices, reception room, chapel, preparation room, workshop and garage. The specialised custom-built hearse and limousine can cost in the region of £55,000 each, new. They are not cheap, nor

would you expect them to be. We are indeed fortunate in this country to have coachbuilders who specialise in the manufacture of funeral vehicles and produce hearses and limousines of a very high quality. Finally, from the moment the family informs the funeral director of the death, he and his staff are involved in the arrangement for maybe the next four or five days. It is just not anyone who can work in this profession; the staff are virtually hand-picked; many go on to gain qualifications and they must receive a comparative remuneration.

Let us now move on to the statutory or mandatory fees. Once the family has decided what form the funeral will take certain fees must be paid on their behalf. If, say, there is to be a cremation, there are fees at the crematorium, and doctors' cremation certificates must be paid for. These certificates authorise the cremation, and if the cremation is to be preceded by a church service, there are fees at the church. If the family have decided on interment/burial there will be fees to pay at a cemetery or churchyard and, again, church fees. Many of these fees will have to be paid on the day of the funeral, the exception being the crematorium who might give a week's credit. As the funeral director is the person who orders all the above services he is responsible for their payment.

Let us now turn to the optional fees. There are items that are not absolutely necessary but are very often required by the family. The funeral director is asked to supply them and they are also included in his account. They can be for floral tributes; notices in local, regional or national newspapers; printing church service sheets; refreshments; meals and sometimes accommodation for people travelling from such a distance that they are unable to return home on the same day. It is not unusual for the mandatory, statutory and optional fees to amount to one third, and in some cases considerably more, of the total account. These fees have to be paid and in most cases it is the funeral director's responsibility. In addition to his own fees, the funeral director must carry the credit for these other fees until the account is settled; in some instances this can be several months. I think it is fair to say that the majority of funeral directors regard this as an occupational hazard but it can be without doubt a severe strain on their financial resources.

If the funeral director is a member of the National Association of Funeral Directors he must give the family a written estimate either at the time the funeral arrangements are made but certainly before the day of the funeral.

I have found, after well over thirty years arranging funerals, that it is not very often that a family has said to me, 'My mother or father has died and we want the cheapest funeral possible.'

They may indicate that they want a simple funeral, and by that they very often mean a funeral without ostentation, but not without quality of service, dignity and respect. What the critics of our profession fail to realise is that a funeral is the last thing a family can be involved in for, say, a much loved mother or father and regard a dignified funeral – and in particular the service – as a tribute to that person. Sometimes a family are short of adequate funds for the funeral. It is then the funeral director's duty to discover if he can arrange the funeral within the given parameters. If this is not possible he will try to determine whether they qualify for assistance, e.g. a payment from the Social Fund.

Whatever the outcome, a funeral director will arrange and conduct that funeral with dignity and respect, regardless of the origin of the fundings. Of course, we have the other end of the scale when a family want the very best funeral money can buy including a coffin or casket of very high quality. I have already mentioned travellers' funerals where this is commonplace; but with other families, too, it has become a tradition to have a funeral with no restraint on expense.

Every so often the subject of DIY funerals comes up. As funeral directors we cannot raise any objection to a family who sincerely wish to personally make their own arrangements, and if required give advice. The families who choose to do this are in the minority, which is just as well for the sake of the funeral directors, but it is a bit like maintaining your own car or handling the conveyancing on the sale of your house – it's considerably safer with a professional motor engineer or a qualified solicitor. It is already a traumatic situation for the family and if something goes wrong it could be devastating. There are hygiene and environmental regulations to be adhered to, plus administrative requirements; and regardless of where the person has died someone has to place them in the coffin. This could be at a hospital or public mortuary and in the presence of other deceased persons. Some people would say money can be saved by a DIY arrangement; I do not think you can argue with that, but someone is having to contribute some time, even with a DIY funeral, so that must be taken into account.

Independent surveys have shown that a funeral director and his staff can be involved for approximately forty hours on an average funeral. A professional will always do a more competent job than an amateur and I have not encountered many families who are prepared to settle for second best for the care of a much loved member of their family. A funeral director is just not there to sell a coffin and turn up on the day of the funeral; he can very often build up a friendly and close relationship with the family during the arrangements, especially if he is dealing with a devastated bereaved partner who seems isolated, has no family or even close friends. In these circumstances it is not unusual for their relationship to continue some considerable time after the funeral.

There will always be some people who will be determined to arrange a funeral themselves, regardless of the difficulties and traumatic circumstances they might experience. If this is really what they want then no one should stand in their way.

I will just finish by saying that as far back as my father and grandfather could go, no member of our family ever participated in the funeral of a close family member. A colleague would always act on their behalf. Since I have been head of the business this tradition has remained unchanged; when my mother and father died two funeral directors who were also friends arranged and conducted the funerals.

About ten years ago some local councils started to talk about setting up their own 'Municipal Funeral Service'. Presumably the intention was to provide cheap funerals by the council, with the original concept of having their own premises and facilities such as Chapels of Rest, their own car fleet and staff. It soon became clear that this was not how it was going to be. The councils were all independent and their services were not identical but one thing they did have in common was that no premises were built or bought, no fleets purchased or funeral directors employed. The municipal service became a tendered or contracted out service to an existing funeral director.

The first problem arose for the ratepayer. If a member of his family died and he felt he might qualify for a council funeral, he had to obtain a voucher from the council offices, which are not open twenty-four hours. If, say, the death occurred at home on a Friday evening it was going to be Monday morning before anything could happen. Obviously this was not going to work and it was quickly changed so that the ratepayer could make direct contact with the contractor, in other words the funeral director. I understand that some councils required payment in advance and even this prerequisite had to be abandoned. Regardless of how low the cost of the funeral is, there are many families who cannot lay their hands on several hundred pounds at a moment's notice. I understand a number of other councils have considered providing their own funeral service but because of financial and in some cases legal constraints decided not to proceed. My own view is that such a service was never required; the majority of funeral directors offer a basic simple funeral anyway. The private funeral director will carry out the removal, if required, without delay and will not demand payment immediately.

People have asked how is it that a funeral director can arrange and conduct a funeral for a local authority cheaper than he can for the general public? Well, it is not unlike selling empty seats on an airliner at a low cost price. If the funeral director's overheads such as fleet, wages and premises are covered by his private funerals and he can then acquire an additional, say, twenty-five funerals per month by reducing his costs he is likely to make a profit, but he certainly would not do so if his reduced-priced funerals had to cover his overheads. Some funeral directors would say that they would have nothing to do with these schemes; but if you are a funeral director and the majority of your work comes from the area where the local authority has set up one of their services, you might well think that the only way to retain your market share would be to tender for the service. To sum up, I do not think that many families see the local authority or council as a satisfactory alternative to their own local funeral director, or will be enamoured of the idea of having to go to the local council officer for a voucher before the arrangements can commence.

On 6th April, 1987, the death grant for funeral expenses ceased. At that time it stood at £30, the figure it had been for twenty years. It had really become an irrelevance, capable of paying only a very small proportion of a funeral account. Everyone was entitled to receive the grant, regardless of whether they required it or not, so it was quite obvious the whole procedure was in need of reform. It was replaced by a payment for funeral expenses from the Social Fund. To qualify for this you had to be in receipt of one of the following: income support, family credit, housing benefit or disability working allowance. Other stipulations included that any money from the deceased's estate, insurance payments and lump sums from pension schemes should be taken into account and deducted from any payment made. Furthermore, savings over £500 would be taken into account and offset against payment.

The funeral payment is intended to help towards the cost of a simple funeral within the UK and as well as the basic requirements it covers the death certificate, flowers from the person arranging the funeral, conveyance of the deceased to where the funeral is to take place, provided it is within the UK, and up to £75 extra costs that might be incurred because of the religion of the deceased. For some reason I never understood it did not cover payment for an obituary notice. If payment is refused the claimants have the right to appeal to an independent Social Security appraisal tribunal. At the onset of the service it was anticipated that those people who were responsible for arranging 10 per cent of all funerals would qualify for Social Fund payments. This did not happen; in fact the take-up rate was extremely low.

In January, 1989, I was asked by the National Association of Funeral Directors if I would be prepared to head a team with two other funeral directors to attend the University of York to assist members of the Department of

Social Policy and Social Work Social Policy Research Unit, who had been authorised by the Social Security Department responsible for funeral payments within the Social Fund, to determine why people eligible for these payments were not applying for them. My colleagues were Victor Fielder and Graeme Skidmore, also members of the National Association of Funeral Directors. At that time Social Security figures had shown that a total of 39,000 people who were eligible for payments from the fund had not applied resulting in £15 million being unclaimed. The consequence of this was that if the Social Security Department could not justify the need for the monies they would be reclaimed by the Treasury. I must just clarify one point here, namely that the money available for funeral payments within the Social Fund was not new money but funds that were originally allocated for the death grant.

After lengthy discussion it was found that the most likely reason that those who were eligible had not taken advantage of the service was lack of publicity. The unit asked us if a survey of our clients during the course of the funeral arrangements would be feasible. We pointed out the difficulties in carrying out any survey at such a sensitive time. It has been my view for some time that if you are trying to determine how the public feel about any aspect of our profession you have to do it without departing from the normal questions you would ask in the course of the funeral arrangements. The public would very soon realise that you were asking specific questions not related to their arrangements and could very quickly become annoyed. We looked at other ways that a survey could be carried out; one suggestion put forward was through the registrars, whose offices every family must attend at some time before or in some cases after the funeral. The unit were even prepared to carry out their own survey but it was estimated that this would take eighteen months and was thought that the time factor might be critical in the dispute between the Department of Social Security and the Treasury. After all that, no survey was carried out by anyone. Leaflets and pamphlets were published and gradually the public became aware of the Social Fund payments. Since that time the provisions have been amended several times, and currently the Department of Social Security is in the process of trying to reduce the amount available to the fund, with constraints on the proportion paid to the funeral director. There is no suggestion at this stage of asking that the numerous agencies the funeral director pays fees to on the family's behalf should take a cut in their fees. It is hardly fair. Not all the aims of the research group were met but I felt the discussions we had were of some benefit. The written report I submitted to the National Association of Funeral Directors gave us a better awareness of the Social Fund payment at its outset. The most positive conclusion in my view was that the National Association of Funeral Directors stated that funds should be available for funeral payments, within the Social Fund, for those in genuine need.

Thankfully the days of the pauper funeral are no more. There has always been provision in this country, certainly in living memory, for people who could not afford to pay for a funeral, and I am sure there always will be. Most people want to be in a position to pay for the funeral themselves. That is the only way that positively guarantees them getting the exact funeral of their choice.

Chapter Eleven

Early in 1983 I received a telephone call from the funeral director, Howard Hodgson, saying he was interested in buying our business and could we meet. My father and I decided that we would be very interested to hear what he had to say. I think by this time nearly everyone in our profession had heard of Howard and the phenomenal growth of his business. Their original funeral business was founded by George Hodgson in the nineteenth century in Birmingham and continued with successive members of the family. In 1923 it became a limited company. Over the years the business expanded and by the early 1960s was arranging about one thousand funerals per year. However, the business gradually declined, probably owing to the drop in population in their area of business as much as anything else. By the early 1970s the business was only arranging about four hundred funerals and was in severe financial difficulties. In 1975 Howard purchased the business from his father.

Howard had worked in the business previously, joining the firm in 1969 but only remaining two years, leaving to pursue a career in insurance. Virtually from the first day in control Howard had to fight to keep the company afloat having to convince the bank not to foreclose. He very soon realised that the only way for the business to survive was to increase the turnover. The death rate was static so the only other way forward was through acquisition. So Howard started to purchase funeral businesses mainly in the

Birmingham area, then gradually he went further afield. By 1986 Hodgsons had a listing on the London Stock Exchange's Junior Market – the unlisted securities market – and had approximately one hundred and fifty offices in six regions: West Midlands, South Wales, East Midlands, South-East, North-East and North-West.

Howard's theory was, given the high level of fixed costs in our profession, that the optimum use of both assets and staff would be the fundamental way to profitability. So he then devised systems to control expenditure which were used to the maximum of the facilities available. The whole operation could only be described as aggressive acquisition. Howard went after small, medium and large sized businesses including in 1987 the House of Fraser Funerals which included over fifty businesses and 13,500 funerals. His style was something the profession in our country had never seen before. He engaged Dennis Amiss, the former test cricket batsman, as director responsible for acquisitions and public relations.

In 1987 he negotiated an agreement with Volvo UK Limited to supply one hundred and thirty Volvo hearses and limousines. The plan was for them to replace all existing fleets. They were all in the new Hodgson colour, midnight blue, with chauffeurs and bearers attired in Portland grey. At that time it was thought to be the largest order for limousines ever placed in the world. In addition all staff at the funeral offices and chapels wore midnight blue suits and all future refurbishment, including furniture, would reflect a corporate image.

My father and I had our first meeting with Howard in March, 1983. He arrived with a small entourage, including a legal adviser. We discussed many aspects of the profession, with of course particular emphasis on our business. He told us what Hodgsons Holdings had achieved so far and his plans for the future. The meeting probably lasted two hours and when he left we agreed to meet again in the near future.

At the second meeting our accountant, David Robinson, was present. We then proceeded into more detail. After that meeting Howard made a provisional bid for the business. We declined and asked for an increased offer. Howard made a new offer and we agreed to another meeting. At this meeting, as well as Howard's people, our accountant, David Robinson, and solicitor, Derek Curtis, were to be present. We all agreed to meet at my office around midday and I had arranged for us to have a working lunch at Fairfield Manor Hotel just outside York. However, Howard and his people arrived about an hour early and he suggested that he and I could go ahead to Fairfield and the others would follow. I always felt that this was a deliberate ploy by Howard to talk to me on my own; not unreasonable, I expect, if he thought there was some advantage for him. However, if you are aware of such a move it can prove to be counter-productive. If I could point at a time when the seeds of doubt crept in about the sale of the business that would have to be it.

Howard was charming, persuasive and an extremely competent businessman but some of the changes he made in the businesses he acquired were so radical that in my view they would be sure to damage at least some of his acquisitions and would have certainly been difficult to implement at J. Rymer. To give you one example, his idea was that at every business one person would be responsible for arranging all the funerals and another colleague would then conduct the funerals. This was totally contrary to our own concept of continuity, where the whole idea is for the funeral director to build up a relationship with the family from the first meeting and continue alongside them throughout the arrangements until the day of the funeral and beyond, if required. But this alone would not have made us change our mind. If you decide to sell your business you have to accept that the new owners are going to have different ideas from your own. Some you will not go along with but others are sophisticated and cost-effective and in the long term make the business more efficient.

At Fairfield that day Howard and I talked for some time on our own with Howard doing most of the talking. My contribution was mainly a bit part. We were joined later by Howard's colleagues and my accountant, David Robinson, and solicitor, Derek Curtis; virtually all the ends were tied up, the price agreed and my own position decided. My father had semi-retired the previous year; my eldest son, Richard, who had joined the business in 1981 would remain and the existing staff would be retained. I was to be a consultant to the business with an office at J. Rymer. Among the items of stock that were in the sale was our large store of timber, which consisted of coffin sets. Shortly after that meeting I received a letter from Howard's solicitors with details of the draft contract for the assignment of goodwill, fixtures and fittings, sale of fleet, etc., but with a rider informing us that their clients would be unable to purchase the timber stock as it would be no use to them. At that time we were buying probably 90 per cent of our coffins, then furnishing them on our own premises; but we always liked to be in the position to set on and make a coffin ourselves if the need be, hence our timber stock. I do not recall the actual value at that time but it would certainly be several thousand pounds.

After further correspondence and a conversation with Howard, he adamantly refused to purchase the timber. Thus if the acquisition was to proceed, we would have to sell the timber ourselves. Maybe that would have not been too easy once we were out of the mainstream of business and we would have probably ended up nearly having to give it away. Howard had a great number of contacts, particularly with coffin manufacturers, and it would have been comparatively easy for him to dispose of the timber. Even extremely clever men have flaws, and this stubbornness over what was to all intent and purposes a very minor item was not the reason we decided not to sell. However, along with other considerations, it was probably the straw that broke the camel's back.

After a lengthy conversation with my father in which he left the final decision to me, I telephoned my accountant, David Robinson, and asked him to inform Howard that we had decided not to proceed with the acquisition. This was the day before completion. Within a very short time I received a telephone call from Howard in which he tried to persuade me to reconsider, even to the extent of purchasing the timber. By this time it was too late. I had decided I did not want to sell to Howard. In the three months I had negotiated with him I had learnt many things from him that benefited me in the years ahead. He was good company and I recognised his achievements but I would not have been happy working for him.

Howard continued for the next few years with his acquisitions. In September, 1989, he merged with Kenyon Securities becoming Britain's largest firm of funeral directors with a market share of 11 per cent. However, high levels of gearing and a considerably lower than forecast mortality rate produced poor figures for the first half of 1990, which meant that the results for the company would be well below what had originally been predicted. By this time the largest shareholder in the new company was the French funeral directors Pompes Funèbres Générales. In January, 1991, Howard resigned as Chief Executive of PFG Hodgson Kenyon International, to someone on the outside. This move was sudden and unexpected but to anyone who knew Howard it was predictable; with the involvement of Kenyons, but more importantly the French, his overall control must have been watered down. It is inconceivable that knowing the direction from which Howard had come, from the brink of receivership in 1975 to Chief Executive of the largest company of funeral directors in the UK, that this most flamboyant of characters could possibly be content unless he was pulling all the strings. He sold his 12.5 per cent stake in PHKI to the French for around £5.9 million and departed.

In retrospect, Kenyons was probably a merger too far. The very size of the company making it vulnerable to a predatory takeover. Howard was not everyone's cup of tea but he gave the profession a long overdue kick up the backside which made a great many of us, if we are honest, take a long hard look at ourselves; and although he did not get everything right, a great many of us benefited from those years when he was involved in our profession.

In 1987 I proceeded down the road to acquisitions, acquiring funeral directors in York and in other towns within a close radius. Between 1987 and 1990 I acquired five firms. The knowledge I gained through my involvement with Howard proved invaluable during this period. There was very little in common with Howard's acquisitions and my own. His were large and numerous, mine small and relatively few. His acquisitions were described as aggressive, mine were positively friendly. In the late 1960s and early 1970s we bought one carriage master and a funeral director and merged them into J. Rymer without trading under their names. Also, as I have mentioned earlier, my father bought Alf Dalton's carriage masters in 1945 when we acquired our first fleet, but these new mergers were totally different; without the name to trade under the work would very quickly disappear.

Families in general are extremely loyal to funeral directors, much as they are to their doctors and solicitors. They do not change unless something goes drastically wrong. As far as I was concerned – and just as important – was keeping the former owners involved in arranging and conducting their own funerals. Families very often remember the person who arranged a previous funeral for them and it would not be unusual for them to request that person again.

It has been suggested that there is maybe something underhand about buying a business and not stating openly the change in ownership. However, if the former owners are still arranging and conducting the funerals with the same staff, as is the case with all my acquisitions, to make a big fuss about the change in ownership could also be misleading and counter-productive to a smooth changeover.

When a large group such as Hodgsons acquired a business it had to fit into the groups work practices, particularly the administration; but with a medium size firm such as my own acquiring a business, it was far easier to absorb others without any great upheaval. The last thing you wanted to do was change how they operated; the one thing you wanted to do was improve the standard of service they provided. For example, you can introduce a more efficient 24-hour service, a modern fleet and more smartly dressed staff, particularly the chauffeurs and bearers. That way the only comment that would be made about any change in business will be positive.

All the businesses I acquired were in a twenty mile radius of York. Our main office and garage is in easy reach of the York bypass and gives us quick access to the branches in the other towns, enabling us to service all of them with hearses and limousines from our main offices and garage.

There are always going to be people who will not approve of a change in ownership of a funeral directors and will go elsewhere. They may also be unhappy because the cost of the funeral has risen, but if you improve the quality of the service you give to such an extent that people comment on it – and they have – I do not think most people would think it unreasonable for there to be some adjustment in the cost to reflect the improvement in the service they receive.

Chapter Twelve

The main trade association representing our profession was founded in 1905, as the BUA, or British Undertakers Association. It changed its name in 1935 to its present day title NAFD, the National Association of Funeral Directors. Some of my colleagues still prefer to call themselves 'undertakers' but the majority of us think that funeral director has a less sinister tone; it currently represents 68 per cent of the funeral directors in the UK. It is allied to many associations and organisations in this country and throughout the world and has had a code of practice since 1907. The current one is monitored by the Office of Fair Trading and it has its own disciplinary and conciliatory committee which rules against any member who is thought to have been in contravention of the Code of Practice. It also looks into any complaints made by the public against any member. Happily there are very few of these. In fact a survey commissioned by the OFT several years ago stated that of the 600,000+ funerals taking place in Britain every year, only about two hundred complaints were received by the trading standards officer.

The Association membership includes large PLCs, medium size firms and 'one-man bands'; at its strongest it represented about 80% of the profession. In the last few years it has had less than a smooth passage with various disputes within the membership which have caused resignations. Happily a great number of these have now returned to the fold.

The NAFD is divided into twenty-one areas, with eighty-one local associations, and in Yorkshire one surviving funeral vehicle owners' section. Each has its own secretary and committee, and a new national president is elected each year. As well as presiding over the business matters in the Association, he or she (we had our first lady president, Pat Bennett, in 1991) will carry out numerous social engagements throughout the country in the year of office and consequently can be absent from their business for a considerable period of time. There is a national council and an executive committee which are each allocated specific responsibilities within the Association. One of these is education, which has a high priority, and members are encouraged to study and sit for the Association's Diploma in Funeral Directing. Among the other areas of responsibility are the Professional Standards Board, Code of Practice and Health and Safety which is extremely important to all funeral service staff. A member of the executive committee is also appointed the Association's public relations officer. This is, in my view, the ultimate of hot seats and without doubt the most demanding job within the Association, but I would say that for nine years I was a public relations officer for the NAFD.

Gradually over the last few years there has been a growing interest in our profession within the media; needless to say, it is not just our profession, it is any profession which draws their attention, particularly if something unpleasant happens. You cannot blame them. They have to fill newspapers and TV companies have to provide documentary current affairs and consumer programmes. A feature recording what an excellent service a funeral director is providing for the local community is not what they want; it will not sell newspapers or keep the public glued to their televisions; but regrettably very often the result is a story so distorted that it is beyond all recognition in relation to the true facts. Of course, sometimes these programmes manage to uncover some scandalous operation along with the villains who run it – not in our profession, I hasten to add. They of course are then to be congratulated but sometimes they get it so wrong that the newspaper is forced to print a retraction, usually in some remote corner of the newspaper. If the TV programme gets it wrong and *they* are forced into a retraction, it usually takes the form of an escalating Dead Sea scroll, with voice to match, following on after, the credits of one of their subsequent programmes, when the majority of viewers probably have dashed off to make a cup of tea: not really good enough.

It is always going to be difficult for a NAFD public relations officer to sound absolutely positive about his profession. If he is defending something or somebody he is on a par with his public relations colleagues in other professions, but if he is attempting to convince people what a first-class job the funeral director and his staff do he is talking about a subject that a lot of people do not want to contemplate and will find it hard to get enthusiastic about. If the media are going to make a programme interesting, or better still for them, controversial, then they have to find something unpleasant. The cost of a funeral is almost certain to drop into this category, usually the emphasis being put on how distasteful it is for anyone to make money from the result of anyone's death.

Another favourite seems to be unethical practice – fair enough if true, but very often distorted beyond all recognition and largely unproven. Then we have the disaster, something that has unhappily gone wrong with the funeral, from the hearse being involved in an accident, the funeral director forgetting to remove an item of jewellery from the deceased, to the worst possible scenario – cremating or interring the wrong person. Of course we all hope and pray that none of these mistakes happen but there are over

600,000 funerals arranged and conducted in this country each year and regrettably sometimes they do. If the media then become involved, what has started out as an accident or a genuine mistake can sound like an act of irresponsible negligence. Of course mistakes should not happen and every responsible funeral director, whether small, medium or large, should have his own procedures to cover every aspect of his work, and then ensure his staff follow them to the letter.

My first encounter with the media occurred during the mid 1960s. My father had arranged a funeral to take place at a Methodist church in the city centre. When the cortège arrived at the church, my father got out of the hearse and was quickly met by the minister. I realised straight away that something was wrong, and it certainly was. Going on in the church at that very time was a large meeting of Methodist ministers. Our minister had quite innocently arranged for the funeral to take place, unaware of the pre-arranged gathering. Our service in church would probably take about twenty minutes, so to us the simple solution seemed to be for the ministers to vacate the church while the funeral service took place. For what reason I do not know this apparently was not feasible. After further discussion and attempts at persuasion it soon became apparent that the service was not going to take place at that church on that day, so two options were put to the family: postpone the funeral until the following day or hold the funeral service elsewhere. They very quickly decided that they did not want a postponement. Family and friends get geared up, for want of a better expression, for a funeral and any delay just makes the whole experience more traumatic than it already is.

By means of several telephone calls, and with the family's approval, the funeral service was re-arranged at another Methodist church about fifteen minutes away. We then set off on our second cortège, arrived at the church and carried the coffin inside for the service. I then came outside whilst the service proceeded. As I came through the door of the church I was approached by a man who identified himself as a reporter from the *Yorkshire Evening Press*. He asked me if I would explain what had happened. This I did. The remainder of the funeral went without a hitch. The family were definitely upset but at least the funeral had taken place on the correct day, albeit considerably later and not at the church of their choice.

It was the account in the *Yorkshire Evening Press* that shook me. The headline was something like, FUNERAL REFUSED ENTRY AT DOOR OF CHURCH, which of course it was. It then went on to recount the whole unfortunate incident along with numerous quotes from yours truly. This was my first lesson in public relations and in particular responding to the media.

It was 1967 before we received the media's attention again. On this occasion a non-contentious topic, the business moving premises for the first time since 1848. My father gave an interview to the *Yorkshire Evening Press*'s reporter, John Blunt, which featured in the paper along with a photograph of Father pictured outside our old premises.

In 1980 an incident occurred at the York Crematorium which hit the headlines. A funeral service had taken place at the crematorium. After the service two members of the family had walked to the rear of the crematorium, looked through some doors and said they had witnessed the member of their family whose funeral service they had just attended, lying on something but not in a coffin, implying that the coffin had been stolen. I do not intend to go into detail other than to say that we were the firm who were unfortunately carrying out the funeral arrangements, and whatever those two people said they witnessed that day it certainly was not a coffin being stolen.

Unfortunately, a court case followed against a member of staff at the crematorium. He was quite rightly found not guilty but for the duration of the trial the funeral directors were regrettably in the wrong kind of limelight. Anyone who was connected to the profession in York knew that these accusations were groundless but you cannot blame some members of the public wondering if there was any truth in the allegations. It emerged after the case that the employee who had been accused had worked at the crematorium since its opening in 1962. He was known personally by nearly everyone connected to the profession in the area, including ministers and priests from all denominations, had an impeccable character and had never ever been in trouble with the law before.

As far as I am aware he never worked again and died soon after. In my view he was destroyed by the whole sorry affair. Although we were not accused of anything we wondered whether our business would be harmed by the publicity. As far as we were aware it was not. During the course of the trial my father appeared as a witness. The fact that at that time he had already been in business fifty-six years, and the comments passed in the judge's summing up regarding his character could not have done us any harm.

In 1985 I received a letter from Andrew Waite, a Leeds funeral director. Andrew had formerly been the secretary of the National Association of Funeral Directors' Yorkshire area and was now a member of the National Executive. He said he proposed to set up a small public relations team to represent the Yorkshire area. The team would consist of Andrew, myself and David Kaye, another Leeds funeral director. I think that if I had been offered any other job in the NAFD I would have turned it down, but public relations was something I was already interested in and felt

I had some ability in that field. So without hesitation I accepted.

In October of that year I attended my first PR education meeting at Leeds. During the course of the meeting we were shown a video of an interview with a funeral director. He was being questioned about several aspects of the profession. The longer the interview went on, the more his ability to respond to the questions deteriorated and it ended in a fiasco. I looked across the room to where my new PR colleague David Kaye was sitting. He was already looking at me. He did not say a word, but the exchanged glances said it all. What have we let ourselves in for? After the meeting Andrew tried to reassure us that all would be well, but our confidence had been shaken.

In November, David and I attended our first PR training seminar in Manchester. It was conducted by Ernest Joyce of Michael Joyce PR Consultants, who represented the Association at that time. Also present were Mary Ellement, our national PR officer, and several other new PR officers. We were taught the basic dos and don'ts of public relations. We also took part in mock one-to-one interviews on various subjects with Ernest acting as interviewer. Although there is nothing like the real thing, this was the nearest most of us had been to an interview and as far as I was personally concerned they gave me the confidence I required when I got involved with the real McCoy.

Not long after the Manchester seminar a person died of the Aids virus in our area. This followed on very closely after the massive publicity surrounding the death of film star Rock Hudson. I think it is fair to say that the majority of people certainly in this country had very little knowledge about the Acquired Immune Deficiency Syndrome (Aids) up until that time and it came as a tremendous shock to discover that a virtually new incurable disease could be sexually transmitted. I know very little about the person who died in our area other than that his family had chosen interment rather than cremation and because of the cause of death the cemetery had refused the interment. If the funeral had been cremation I do not think there would have been a problem. I never knew the funeral director or the cemetery the family had chosen.

My first knowledge of the incident came with an unofficial telephone call informing me that the media had got hold of the story and it was about to break. Within half an hour it certainly did and my first real test as a public relations officer for the National Association of Funeral Directors was under way. During the course of the following two hours I gave telephone interviews to local, regional and national newspapers and one news agency. It seemed to me as if I was the only one responding to the story. I was not even sure that the funeral director involved was a member of the NAFD. Later that day I received a telephone call from Andrew Waite, the senior member of our PR team. He virtually said, 'What the hell is going on?' I proceeded to bring him up to date, telling him how I had been informed of the incident and at the same time saying how little I really knew about the people involved.

One of the first things I was taught about public relations was that if you have to defend something or somebody you have enough on responding for your own people without doing it on someone else's behalf. This was such an incident; it was the cemetery authority that was refusing to inter the person in their cemetery, not the funeral director, and it would have been very easy to say, 'Sorry nothing to do with us.' But of course I could not do that; I had to sound sympathetic, which indeed I genuinely was. As I have already said at that time we still knew very little about Aids and the cemetery probably thought that if someone was interred in their cemetery with this disease the ground would be contaminated for ever. This is not the case, but ten years on we are now better informed. Eventually the funeral did take place but where and what form it took I am not sure. The story even appeared on one or two of the front pages of national newspapers which reflected the interest the case aroused.

Just a footnote to this incident. Near to York Station and just beyond the old city walls lies a small burial ground. All the people there are the victims of a cholera outbreak in the city in 1832. As far as I am aware that burial ground can never be disturbed as it is recognised that even after all these years the disease could still be contagious.

Over the nine years I was a public relations officer I gave newspaper, radio and TV interviews, the majority on contentious issues which is the nature of the thing. Some on subjects allied to my own profession, e.g. private burial grounds, or DIY funerals and very occasionally something a little more light-hearted. For example, in 1988 Graeme Skidmore, Vic Fielder and myself appeared on a programme for BBC Radio York called *Just Another Day*, in which among other things we recalled some humorous incidents we had experienced as funeral directors.

In recent years we have gradually seen the emergence of the televised police press conference, which very often follows a disaster or a murder. We see paraded before us on our television screens relatives of the victims or victim of some terrible incident very often parents of a murdered child, appealing for help in apprehending the person or persons responsible. These people are experiencing distress and trauma that most of us we pray to God will never have to go through. I have, thank goodness, personally never experienced it but through my work I have been in close contact with families who have. It is hard enough to try to come to terms with such tragedy with your family and friends around you but to be then persuaded to appear before television cameras and reporters with the knowledge that the nation is watching your every move and hanging on to your every word must pile agony on agony.

When someone dies, particularly if the circumstances are sudden or violent, the family will really try to do anything they are asked, if they are persuaded that in some way it will help the police and authorities. In some cases children are asked to appear. Just recently a young girl who had discovered her murdered friend's body appeared at one of these conferences. She was crying, terrified and quite obviously distressed and I wonder what long-term effect this kind of additional unnecessary experience can have.

I think it is way past the time we analysed the results of these conferences to see if there are any beneficial results coming from them and if there are not, as I suspect, to then look for a serious alternative to these painful shows. Sometimes it is even worse. Families are persuaded to take part in a police press conference when there is not even a pretence that it will help anyone, when there is no suspect to find or help required from the public but somehow they have been persuaded to relive their dreadful experience again in front of the nation. If it is deemed really necessary that an appeal to the public would be of great advantage in particular cases, then why not use a lady police officer, with the emphasis on 'lady'. Regardless of their ability, male police officers very seldom, in my view, come across in a suitable way in these circumstances. I think what I am trying to say is that when members of a family are persuaded to appear, they are so quite obviously distressed that the public may only be concentrating on the state of those people rather than what they are saying, which misses the whole point of the exercise.

Of course funeral directors are not experts on police press conferences but we do know something about bereavement and how it affects people. We see it every day and I think we have a right to comment on something that in my view makes the situation worse rather than better.

As I write it is a month since the terrible incident at Dunblane. Prior to the funerals there was an appeal for the media to let the families have the funerals privately. As far as I am aware the majority of the media acceded to these requests, but at least one tabloid newspaper published photographs. What a pity. In York we have a procedure with our local newspaper, the *Yorkshire Evening Press*. If someone dies who is a well-known York or district citizen, or if someone dies as a result of an accident, they very often want to feature a story. Rather than just go away and indulge in guesswork they use the funeral directors as a go-between. The press contact him and he asks the family on their behalf whether they are prepared to give an interview. If not, that is it; but if they are prepared to talk to the press, then the funeral director will pass on the family's telephone number to the reporter for him or her to contact them and it seems to work very well.

I was in Mexico on holiday at the time of the Oklahoma City Federal Building bombing and consequently saw the extensive coverage of the atrocity on American TV. Thankfully, the USA has very little experience of domestic violence of this nature, whereas we in the UK have been dealing with it for nearly thirty years. The worst scenes in the TV coverage at Oklahoma City were of the dead and injured being brought out of the building, especially the children. However, the press conferences that were held in the days following the incident were handled extremely professionally. The thing that really impressed me was the ability of the people who responded to the questions asked by the media. These included Gary Mares (Oklahoma Fire Department), Weldon Kennedy (FBI agent in charge), James Lee Witt (FEMA Director of the Federal Emergencies Management Agency) and finally the most impressive of them all, Attorney-General Janet Reno.

Any questions that were asked and thought not to be relevant were not answered. If a question was asked that they were not prepared to answer they politely said, 'I cannot answer that at this time, next question,' and the questioner seemed to accept it. These people held very responsible jobs and at the same time possessed the public relations expertise to respond to the media in such a professional way. I expect what I am trying to say is that it was not a show; the sole purpose of the conferences was to give the American people as much information that was possible about a national tragedy without any distractions. The participants would not allow themselves to be intimidated by any of the questions and *they* controlled the direction the press conferences went, not the media.

During my time as a public relations spokesman for the NAFD, with the exception of the very few light-hearted interviews I gave, I had to somehow strike a balance with what I said, and on TV what facial expressions I used in response to the questions. I did not want to give the impression that I was 'a miserable so-and-so' but on the other hand if I smiled too much or – heaven forbid – laughed, you could be sure someone would say that I was not showing respect. Of course, death is not humorous and it should be treated with respect and dignity but sometimes something happens that makes someone smile or even laugh, and although you are a funeral director and traditionally everyone expects you to look miserable, you have to smile with them. If you do not, you could possibly make them feel guilty.

Over the years I have seen many people smile or laugh at a funeral. It can relieve tension and help them through the proceedings. I am sure most of us in this country have seen televised coverage of funerals throughout the world, scenes of distraught emotion, mass crowds, unrelenting wailing and in some cases people being trampled underfoot. What effect this actually has on the immediate members of the deceased's family I shudder to think. It might well be the tradition in that particular country for the people to hold their funeral ceremonies in this fashion, but it is difficult to see how it can be of any comfort to the family. By way of complete contrast, in our country it is the tradition for a funeral to be held with dignity, respect and, apart from the funeral service, in virtual silence. Even our state funerals take this form.

It is always very sad when a much loved member of the family dies but over the years I have arranged funerals of people, very often young people, in the most tragic of circumstances. The most distressing of all involve the death of children. I sincerely have never ceased to be amazed how families seem to cope with this most dreadful period in their lives with such dignity.

The most pleasant and enjoyable aspect of being an NAFD public relations officer I found was when I was asked to speak at meetings or dinners, such as Round Table, Rotary or Women's Institutes. I could be fairly sure that the secretary or organiser of such meetings, when writing to me to ask if I was able to speak, would always make sure that my talk would not be too depressing or even gruesome. Of course I cannot speak for all funeral directors but I am sure the majority of them when speaking on such occasions give an informative talk about their profession at the same time keeping it light-hearted and even humorous.

I resigned as a PR officer for the NAFD in 1994 after nine years. I learnt a tremendous amount during my tenure and always regarded it as a great responsibility to be representing my colleagues. As far as I am aware I did not let anyone down. I am still invited to speak at meetings and dinners and always enjoy it. As with my PR talks the question and answer period at the end of the talk are usually the most amusing at the same time with people showing a genuine interest in what goes on within our profession.

Chapter Thirteen

I expect if I had to name one thing that is associated with our profession and was not around when I started it would have to be the emergence of bereavement counselling. I expect the most recognisable organisation is Cruse which was founded in 1959, originally to help widows. It has now broadened its work to help anyone who has been bereaved. It has about five thousand people working in over one hundred and seventy branches. They are all volunteers, and I understand that there is no other organisation of its kind in the world.

Anyone wishing to train as a counsellor will in the first instance attend a series of lectures on certain topics such as theory of loss and grief, 'loss of a partner', 'loss of a parent', 'loss of a child', suicide, and religious, cultural, ethical and humanistic factors. All these lectures are given by doctors, solicitors, people from different departments of the social services, ministers of religion and funeral directors. Recently I gave one of the lectures. A full course of the lectures lasts about two months. At the conclusion, those who wish to go on to become counsellors will declare their interest. If they are accepted they will go on to further training.

It is very difficult to ascertain how people are going to react to bereavement. The most 'natural' death is that of a parent or partner who lives a long life and then dies peacefully, let's say an elderly father or mother; but if that death is proceeded by a long painful illness there can be very different feelings among the survivors. In the latter instance there can be a great sense of relief that it is all over, that there is no more pain and they no longer have to witness the suffering; and then you can have someone who is considerably younger who has also suffered a long terminal illness. The feelings then can be a mixture between wanting them to be out of their pain but at the same time being so aware that they should not be dying at such a young age.

I have a friend whose wife had a particularly distressing terminal illness. She was nursed in hospital, then in the latter stages at home. Towards the end all he wanted was for her to die peacefully and when she did it was a great relief; but in the months that followed her death he told me that he had feelings of guilt recalling what he had wished for during those weeks preceding her death. It culminated with him wanting her back under any circumstances, including her suffering and him having to watch her suffering.

Then there is the other extreme, namely sudden death, which can take several forms: 'accidents', road accident or an accident at work. Someone leaves home in robust health, there is an accident and they never return. If a member of your family is ill you are probably partly prepared, but with accidents there is no warning. Of course, sudden deaths can take place at home, such as a death from a coronary thrombosis. If that person has not shown any symptoms of heart disease prior to the first attack and they die before any medical help can reach them, the effect on the family, particularly anyone who might be there when the attack takes place, can be traumatic.

So what do Cruse and similar organisations tell us about bereavement and in their view the importance of counselling? They tell us that there are four stages of grief:

Coxwold circa 1930. From where James Rymer left for York 1848.

Coxwold present day.

James Rymer (1813-1898) obituary from the Yorkshire Evening Press-January 1898.

Extract from ledger 1910.

Funeral of Robert Percy Dale (Town Clerk) at St Philip and St James Church, Clifton, York, 27th March 1906 .

John Thomas Rymer (Grandfather, 1878-1925). He is located to the extreme right of the picture.

Advertisement for J. Rymer, circa 1930.

Father (John H. Rymer, 1909-1992) conducting the funeral of
Thomas Lawson, Groundsman for York Rugby League Club, on
7th February 1933.

Funeral of the Reverend Reginald Gaynesford Pyne on 14th February 1934. He was Rector of St Cuthberts Church, York from 1910 to 1934. The funeral was held at St Cuthberts Church and was conducted by the Bishop of Whitby.

The workshop at 35 St Andrewgate in the shadow of York Minster.

The original premises at 35 Andrewgate prior to demolition in 1967.

Father (John H. Rymer, 1909-1992) outside 35 St Andrewgate prior to moving to Penley's Grove Street in 1967.

Premises at Penley's Grove Street, York. Present day.

Premises at Penley's Grove Street, York - present day, showing the author and his sons, all of whom are current operators of the business

Bamforth comic postcard.

1. Shock and disbelief.

2. Expression of grief.

3. Depression and apathy.

4. Signs of recovery.

They point out the many practical problems people can face after the death of a wife, husband or partner. If the person who dies is the one who has been responsible for handling all the finances, the person that is left can literally panic at the thought of having to write a cheque or go into a bank. So the combination of losing your partner and the sudden realisation that you are now going to be responsible for all the finances and paperwork can fill you with trepidation. Alternatively, if the person who dies has been the practical member of the partnership, for example, being responsible for wiring plugs, changing a fuse or tending the garden, the same feeling can arise. Probably the worst scenario of all is if the partner who died has been totally responsible for the cooking and preparation of meals. If you cannot even boil an egg it has to be a real problem and there is of course the business of washing clothing and housework. The ideal thing would be for all couples to learn each other's roles but in the real world that does not happen. Finally, the person who is left is probably going to be living and sleeping on their own for the first time in their lives.

Bereavement counsellors tell us there is a need to mourn and for many people I am sure that this is so, but everyone has to come to terms with bereavement in their own way. My own personal view is that no one, however well intentioned, should seek to impose their solution on anyone else's grief unless invited. It is a mistake to assume that everyone has to grieve. However much someone has loved a person, sometimes, regardless of the circumstances of their death, they are able to accept what has happened, put it behind them and get on with their lives without mourning and the aid of bereavement counsellors. Others are able to find solace through religion and some with just the plain simple presence of family and friends. If they do not grieve they are not callous and will probably choose to remember the person who has died in private moments on their own.

There are certain circumstances when bereavement counsellors seem to be automatically on the scene, for instance in emergencies such as the Piper Alpha oil rig fire, the sinking of the *Herald of Free Enterprise* and the King's Cross tube disaster. I am sure that they will do some very worthwhile work on these terrible occasions but it will not be everyone who will want their attention, and regrettably in some cases it will be counter-productive.

We as funeral directors are expected during the course of making the funeral arrangements to assess whether that family might require the services of a bereavement counsellor. On very rare occasions over my years arranging funerals has it occurred to me that someone who I am talking to might require such help. If it has it has most likely been a person who, during the course of making the arrangements, you discover not only has no family but appears not to have any friends. But for a funeral director to say, 'Do you want me to put you in touch with a bereavement counsellor?' is running a great risk of offending the client. Yet the funeral director, without being aware of it, is probably the first bereavement counsellor. While sitting there making the funeral arrangements it is one of the most natural things for the funeral director to engage in conversation with the family about the person who has died and I must confess that on several occasions I have left a family's home after making the arrangements and have sincerely thought that I have helped them with just a plain and ordinary conversation. To this must be added the fact that maybe making the arrangements had not been such an ordeal as they had envisaged. I have always tried to find an alternative to saying 'I am sorry' when a person has died. No matter how sincere, some people, in my view, might think it strange for a funeral director to be expressing regret about something which, had it not occurred, he would not have a job to do. However, if a family are kind enough to entrust you with personal details about the person who has died, including on occasion some harrowing details, it is extremely hard not to say, 'I am sorry,' and I still find myself saying it.

Some people associated with our profession believe that it is a good thing for children to be involved with death; that they should not be shielded from any aspect of it, and in fact they should be encouraged to become involved if a member of the family dies.

A few years ago, the York funeral directors had an article in the *Yorkshire Evening Press* publicising our profession, the help we can give and explaining in general the work of the funeral director. One of the points we made was how important it was for funeral directors to have a twenty-four hour service so they can immediately respond when contacted by the public. We stressed in particular how important it was that if someone died at home that we were in a position to carry out a removal from the house to the Chapel of Rest at a time the family wanted. The article went on to explain that very often if children lived at the same house it was quite likely that parents or guardians wanted the removal effected as soon as possible. Shortly after the article appeared the press published a letter from a prominent member of the nursing profession in the city saying that children should not be shielded from death and on the contrary should be encouraged to be involved. Now

I recognise that any decision of this nature must be the responsibility of the parents or guardians, but it is my own personal view that it is more natural for children to grow up gradually learning about death along with the many other things in life, pleasant and unpleasant, which they have to know about, rather than thrusting death prematurely at them at such a young age.

During my years as a funeral director people have related stories to me of when they were young, being literally forced into a room to view a member of their family in a coffin, most probably a grandparent, and then being told to kiss them goodbye. This experience had stayed with them for the remainder of their lives and they were determined not to ever let their own children be in the same situation.

I know that you cannot hide death from children, nor would it be sensible to do so, but the level of involvement must depend on the age of the child, its temperament and any indication of its own whether or not it wants to be involved. To go to the other extreme and totally exclude the child from anything concerning the death could give it the feeling of being left out and could also do harm. Children and their relationship with death is always going to be a very delicate issue and never easy.

I hesitate to criticise anything or anybody who seeks to give help to anyone who is trying to come to terms with a bereavement, but it seems to me that we are moving towards a position where many people are going to assume that when someone dies bereavement counselling will follow automatically. The consequence of that may well be that they will not then be able to cope in the future with any subsequent events without outside help. My own personal view is that I am convinced in the majority of cases the most natural way to cope with bereavement is with the comfort of family and friends.

Finally there is another aspect of counselling which concerns me. It seems now to be automatically available to police officers, firemen and medical personnel, particularly if they have been involved in a nasty incident. I apologise if this sounds callous, but why? Funeral directors spend their life at the sharp end of some very tragic events and as far as I am aware I have never heard of them requiring counselling. There have always been disasters and tragic incidents. The police, fire service and medical personnel got on with it and eventually went home and, if they were anything like me, just thanked God that, dreadful as the incident had been, it had not involved me and my family. Any suggestion to them that they required someone to discuss the experience with would most likely have been treated with disdain.

People who enter these professions do so because they think they can do the job, and there are many people who could not; but if they require counselling every time they are involved in a traumatic experience they are in the wrong job and something is amiss. The truth is they probably do not require counselling but someone is telling them they do.

It also seems there is something else emerging. Counselling can be closely followed by compensation. As I have already said there are some instances when counselling can play its part; but what concerns me is if we are moving to a position in the future where not only the public but the professionals are going to have a total dependency on counselling to get them over all the unpleasant but nonetheless natural experiences in life.

Chapter Fourteen

Whenever there is a disaster such as the sinking of the ferry *Herald of Free Enterprise*, the oil rig Piper Alpha, the escalator fire at King's Cross tube station, the pleasure boat *Marchioness* on the Thames and any aviation disaster, everyone – the emergency services, the media and public – quite rightly concentrate on the survivors of these dreadful incidents. Once it is clear there are no more survivors then the task begins of recovering the victims.

One of the most experienced organisations in the world in this field is KES, Kenyon Emergency Services, along with its sister company, KAT, Kenyon Air Transportation. KES acts on behalf of carriers, insurance companies and governments, nationally and internationally. They attended their first civil aviation disaster at Croydon Airport in 1929.

KES's main responsibility is the recovery, identification and repatriation of victims of major disasters. Their highly trained specialist staff have dealt with the aftermath of shipping and oil rig accidents, fires, rail crashes and natural disasters. They have also assisted the police in gathering evidence in several renowned murder cases.

The most significant change that has taken place in aviation disasters since KES attended its first one in 1929 is the carrying capacity of the airliners. The first commercial airliners maximum load would probably have been no more than thirty or forty passengers, whereas today two or three hundred or more is not uncommon and we are not so very far away from airliners that will carry double that amount.

The consequence of this is that when an accident occurs a massive recovery operation is required. By far the largest recovery KES was involved in in the early days was the dirigible airship R101 at Beauvais, France, in 1930, when there were forty-eight victims. Contrast that with the Turkish airliner DC10 at Ermonville, France, in 1974, 345 victims; the Air India Boeing 747 off Cork in 1985, 329 victims; the PanAm Airways Boeing 747 at Lockerbie in 1988, 270 victims, and you become aware of how dramatically KES has had to adapt over the years to modern aviation disasters.

When KES, whose headquarters are in London, receive the first telephone call within minutes the whole organisation is put on red alert. KES comprises two separate teams: the home team, and the field team. Immediately the home team will open its incident operations room and their first task is to accumulate as much relevant information in these early stages as they can for the KES director in control of the field team. Once this information is received the director can make a decision on the level of the KES response. The home team is responsible for assembling the professional members of the field team which consist of pathologists, odontologists, forensic scientists, photographers and embalmers.

The conveyance of the field team to the site of the incident is usually organised by the carrier involved. If for any reason that is not possible KES will make their own independent arrangements. When the field team have left for the site, the home team begin to gather identification data, i.e. dental charts, medical records, fingerprints, registration details and clothing and jewellery descriptions and, at the same time if possible, to determine the families' wishes as to funeral arrangements. This work is carried out by trained experts in this field. It is better for all concerned that this work is done as quickly as possible. The home team can be set up at different locations that can include the accident site or the carrier's base country if necessary.

It is not an unnatural reaction for many of the families of the victims to want to go to the scene of the accident immediately to be close to their relatives. They quite naturally wish to determine what caused the accident and ultimately to bring their relatives home. As much as everyone involved in the recovery wants to do everything that is humanly possible to help the families, there are several reasons why they must be discouraged, at least for the first few days. It is extremely likely that most international airlines are carrying passengers from many different nationalities. One of the home team's and its international agents' priorities is to contact relatives of the deceased as soon as possible, to enable them to gather very necessary and specific information which is vital in the identification of the victims.

If they just jump on the first available plane to the scene it is more than likely that they will leave this information at home, thus prolonging the emergency services' work. Very often air disasters take place in remote locations where there is very limited accommodation. In these circumstances any influx of large numbers of people could cause real problems. Finally, if relatives do manage to arrive at the scene of the disaster you have to determine what affect this will have on them. The television news pictures we get at home when such a disaster occurs in no way conveys a veracious picture of the extent of the devastation at the scene, nor should they. For relatives to witness carnage at close hand in my own view is likely to do more harm than good and might well prolong their ability to recover from such a dreadful experience.

The home team, based in London, is the centre for communications for the entire operation. They are responsible for the provision of information to the media and all enquiries and are the direct link with the field team. It is vital that nothing impedes their work. In complete charge of the field team is a KES director who is responsible for communicating with relatives, police, government departments, local authorities and any other interested parties. He is also responsible for diplomatic liaison and will have considerable experience in responding to the media. The field team are flexible and are able to take on any practical work, including supplementing the labour of workers who are available at the site.

Personnel of the KES mortuary team are chosen for their experience. They are all fully qualified members of BIE, the British Institute of Embalmers, and are fully prepared to travel any where in the world immediately they are informed of the incident.

KES retains the services of some world renowned forensic odontologists and, depending on the size of the response required, several will travel to the scene to carry out the very important task of dental examination of the victims for identification purposes. They will work closely with local authorities and police. In addition an odontologist is based in London with the home team to receive and interpret information from the scene as well as ante-mortem dental records from the relevant countries throughout the world.

Several Home Office pathologists are available at short notice if required to assist in post-mortems for legal and identification purposes.

An experienced photographer with a background in crime work with the police will accompany the team, whose main duty will be to collect visual records of the scene, including victims and property that is recovered. The field team takes responsibility for work in five major areas.

1. Recovery of the victims and preparation of the evidence.

2. Identification of the evidence.

3. Sanitisation and restoration of the victims.

4. Arrangements for repatriation and/or funerals of the victims.

5. Recovery and restoration of personal and other effects.

In the United Kingdom the recovery of the victims is handled by the police and the emergency services. However, in other countries the procedures are governed by local rules and customs. There are many factors, for example local terrain and proximity to populated areas, which affect the efficiency and speed at which the victims are recovered. It may take a few days before the recovery team arrives at the scene, and during that period the local authorities may have started to recover some of the victims. It is quite understandable that out of respect for the dead they should want to do so rather than leave them at the scene of the disaster, but in doing so they have probably disturbed or at worst destroyed vital evidence of identification. In some cases they destroy evidence which might have contributed to establishing the cause of the disaster. In certain countries it is the custom for the disposal of the dead to take place within twenty-four hours. If burial has taken place diplomatic pressure may have to be used to permit the exhumation and post-mortem examination of the victims to fulfil indispensable medical, legal, scientific and sociological requirements.

The identification of the victims can very often be a slow process. In some cases it may take several months and this quite understandably can cause great distress to relatives. Regrettably, some are never identified. To keep the families informed of any progress that is made requires someone with patience and immense understanding of the dreadful trauma they are experiencing. Quite naturally some family members want to see their relative but very often the bodies may be burnt and mutilated to such an extent that personal identification is impossible. In addition, the majority of families will already be experiencing great distress and emotion and to then see their relative with the terrible injuries they may have sustained would only add to their anguish.

Again, this is where it is essential that the person who is the liaison between the family and the emergency services can compassionately discourage them from this course of action. In general the field team director will earnestly try to discourage any personal identification of the victims for the sole reason of sparing the relatives' distress. At the same time he will attempt to persuade the local authorities that with the emergency team's scientific expertise, personal identification is not necessary. He will also present evidence of identification to the Coroner or his equivalent in whatever country the disaster has taken place for his approval.

It is imperative that the field director maintains close contact with the police, medical, local authorities and Interpol. In general, regardless of whatever country the field team operates in, they enjoy close Cupertino with these people who appreciate their expertise and skill in this unpleasant work.

Identification is determined by the following.

1. Forensic odontology is by far the most reliable means of identification of disaster victims. Teeth are able to withstand massive injuries, including fire, which the rest of the body cannot, and the comparison of dental records of the victims with the results of post-mortem examinations means a positive identification is very often conclusive.

2. Documents: if they have survived the disaster, these can help with identification, but to a lesser degree because they are very often inconclusive for instance, passport and airline tickets; it is not unknown for a passenger to be travelling under an assumed name or using someone else's ticket, so it is essential that this evidence is corroborated. Men are more likely to be identified by documents than women because they will carry documents in their pockets along with their wallet. A lady's documents will be in her handbag which is very likely to be lost on impact.

3. Jewellery can greatly assist in the identification of victims. Much of it is made from heat-resistant metals and stones which can survive intensive fire. Jewellery may be inscribed and hallmarks can identify the country of origin. Both the home and field teams have a comprehensive brochure containing many designs of rings, chains and other pieces, to enable relatives to describe items accurately.

4. Fingerprints also assist the team in identification. The KES team have skills in acquiring fingerprints under the most difficult conditions.

5. Physical identification: a post-mortem examination will be carried out on every victim by one of the home team pathologists retained by KES. This can reveal any disease or condition which that person might have had and then when compared with medical case histories by the KES home team may hopefully reveal evidence of identification.

6. DNA: every cell in our body contains DNA (deoxyribonucleic acid). Every human is different, therefore the DNA in one person is different from any other. If samples of DNA are required, the home team are responsible for obtaining samples from the victim's close relatives. The field team will obtain samples from the victims. It is then hoped that the forensic scientists can form a genetic picture. KES are pioneers in the development of this method for the identification of victims of mass disasters.

After all this work is completed, sanitisation and restoration is required. This procedure must comply with public health and international regulations for repatriation. If restoration of the remains is possible to the extent that the family are able to see them, if they so wish, it can contribute to the lessening of distress; but if the field team advise that seeing the victim would not be in the best interests of the family they should be seriously persuaded to accept their professional advice.

Repatriation may not take place as quickly as the families would like but the very nature of a disaster, that is, the infrequency of them, can mean that the authorities are dealing with an incident and the subsequent documentation for the first time. The field team must establish with the relatives what form the funeral will take when the remains are returned home, e.g. interment or cremation, so the correct documentation can be prepared. The field team are conversant with regulations throughout the world with regard to disposal of remains and will be doing their utmost to attain a speedy conclusion so that the remains can be returned home as soon as possible.

Sometimes relatives of a victim will decide against repatriation and request that the funeral takes place locally. That funeral will be arranged by the KES director in conjunction with the carrier's representative and the local authorities.

Regrettably, some of the victims remain unidentified and in these circumstances a mass burial has to be arranged in the country where the disaster has taken place. The KES director will more than likely be responsible for the co-ordination of this complex arrangement. First it will be necessary to secure a suitable site. Labour must be obtained to excavate the grave and landscape designers must be engaged. Transport and accommodation must be provided for relatives, official representatives and the media and then arrangements made for a ecumenical funeral service.

If necessary the field team will obtain authority from the local police to acquire possession of all personal effects and clothing recovered from the disaster on behalf of the underwriters. Articles that are severely damaged along with stained and torn clothing are meticulously searched and then destroyed primarily because they can be a health and fire hazard. A list of all unidentified property is compiled and copies circulated to all relevant parties to enable claims to be made. If it is deemed necessary a display of items can be arranged for personal inspection. Jewellery will be professionally cleaned and restored if possible before being handed back to relatives.

The utmost discretion is required with the handling of documents that are recovered intact, e.g. private diaries and letters. KES have considerable skill and experience in making absolutely sure that they are delivered into the appropriate hands. All passports, domestic and foreign, are returned to the passport officer or relevant government department. Receipts are required for every article that is returned. After an appropriate period of time has elapsed, unclaimed articles are disposed of under instructions from the insurance companies.

All information with regard to the funerals is compiled by the KES home and field teams and this is passed on to the carrier and the relevant local authorities to enable official attendance to be arranged in the countries involved. They will also arrange for floral tributes if required. The victims' remains will have already been transported to their respective countries by the quickest means which is of course by air in a hermetically sealed coffin or casket. If the incident occurs at home, road or air transport may be used. The KES team will if required compile all documentation relating to victims' identification for presentation to the official accident commission. In addition a detailed report is prepared which states the specific cause of death of each victim. All this information can contribute to the accident commission's main function which is to determine why and how the accident occurred and hopefully provide vital knowledge for the future of air safety. All the senior members of the team are experienced in legal technicalities and procedures and are able to provide evidence in court if required.

During my career I have had to arrange funerals of people who have died as a result of air disasters as well as people who have died in traffic accidents abroad. After the family have recovered from the initial shock, their main priority is for their relative to be brought home as soon as possible and for the funeral arrangements to be made, but very often this is not possible. As I have explained earlier, much has to be done including a considerable amount of documentation. I can recall on several occasions the family contacting me sometimes daily to see when their relative was coming home and asking me to commence funeral arrangements.

Experience has taught funeral directors that it is folly to make any arrangements until the remains have arrived in this country. Sometimes under emotional pressure from the family a funeral director has gone ahead and made arrangements because he has been informed that the remains will probably arrive on an unconfirmed flight, and then the flight is postponed or cancelled. The consequence is that the funeral arrangements have to be postponed and this just compounds the distress for the family. Of course, the family want their relative home but the funeral director for the sake of the family must resist the understandable pressure he may be submitted to.

Finally, I must have a special mention for embalmers. Although I am not one myself I have throughout my career recognised the invaluable work they do in our profession. I do not intend to go into detail about the unpleasantness of decomposition but in every working day of our profession embalmers are involved in extremely skilful and in some circumstances difficult work and their profession is largely unsung. After a disaster of any kind, without their expertise the recovery and restoration of the victims would be impossible. The main function of KAT, Kenyon Air Transportation, sister company to KES, is the worldwide repatriation of human remains. They can be responsible for bringing someone home who has just died naturally maybe on holiday, or mass repatriation as a result of a major disaster. They have a network of three hundred and fifty international agents in over one hundred countries. KES have consultants who provide advice to airlines, shipping and oil companies, governments and other emergency services. They also hold training seminars on a regular basis; one was held in Yorkshire recently which my son, Richard, and I attended. Thankfully, major disasters are infrequent, but when one does occur there is an extremely competent and professional organisation ready to respond.

Just a footnote: I know it is probably the last thing you all want to think about before travelling abroad on holiday or business but in the extremely unlikely event that you died by accident or natural causes whilst abroad it does make sense to ensure that your insurance cover would at least bring you back to this country if this is what you would want.

I have on several occasions endeavoured to arrange funerals with families where someone has died abroad and was not insured to be returned home. On one occasion it cost the family several thousand pounds. I expect you could say they were lucky they had the money. If a family cannot raise the funds the alternative would be a funeral in the country where the death took place. If that is not what they want, it can be extremely distressing.

Chapter Fifteen

One of the most significant developments to take place in our profession in recent years is the emergence of pre-arranged and prepaid funeral plans. They have been prevalent in the USA for quite a number of years. Recently there has been a steady increase of pre-planning with families in this country, but if we go back to the very early days of my career, I can remember on the odd occasion people coming to see my father and asking if he could tell them how much a funeral would cost because they were worried that when they died there would not be sufficient funds to pay for the funeral, and even in those days the thought of a pauper or public funeral greatly concerned them. So my father would somewhat reluctantly find out what kind of funeral they wanted and work out the cost. The people would then draw the money out of the bank or retrieve it from under the bed, come back to the office and hand it to my father. He would record the details of the proposed funeral and hand the person a receipt. The first thing my father would say to the person, particularly if they were on their own, was please inform someone of what you have done; if not when something happens to you (he meant died) no one will be aware of your wishes and all this will be to no avail. Of course many people insure their lives but, depending on the level of insurance they have taken out, sometimes there may not be sufficient funds to meet the cost of the funeral.

With a funeral prepayment plan you are able to cover all eventualities. In effect, you are able to arrange the funeral of your choice. It covers the place where the service is to be conducted; the form the service will take, regarding the hymns or readings; whether cremation or interment is desired; and selecting the crematorium or cemetery, choosing a specific grave space if so desired. You might even want to name the venue where your family and friends have a meal after the funeral. When you are sure that the proposed arrangements are to your satisfaction, the funeral director will explain the outlay required.

The charges will be in two parts: the funeral director's fees and the expenses paid on your behalf by the funeral director to other parties, e.g. cemetery, crematorium, church and minister. In addition there may be flowers, press notices and catering costs. This is the only area where additional charges might arise in the future. You may pay these costs at today's prices, say a total of £200, but if there is a 25 per cent increase in the retail price index (RPI) between the time of arranging and the funeral, the plan would cover an increase up to £250. If the cost exceeded that a further charge would have to be made at the time of the funeral. These costs are completely out of the funeral director's hands. The funeral director's own charges are fully itemised and guaranteed with no more payment required whatsoever.

The majority of companies involved with the plans are members of the National Association of Pre-Paid Funeral Plans (NAPFP) The money is deposited in a funeral trust and is guaranteed by a custodian trustee. For example, my own company runs two schemes, 'Dignity ' and 'Chosen Heritage'. The custodian trustee for them both is Barclays Bank plc but the same ground rule still applies as it did all those years ago: tell someone what you have done. Even if you do not want to tell your family, inform your solicitor so that your wishes are complied with.

Just recently I heard of an instance where someone had died on holiday abroad. He had never informed his family that he had pre-arranged his funeral. I expect eventually the documentation would have turned up but by that time it might have been too late. Fortunately, the funeral director read the account of the man's death in the newspaper and knew by this time that he should have been contacted by the family if everything was going to plan. He got in touch with the family and eventually everything went ahead as planned.

With the majority of plans there are no age or health restrictions. If you decide to live in another part of the country the plan can be transferred and you may pay in full or by instalments. Obviously not everyone would want to pre-arrange their own funeral but for those who do the modern funeral plans are a very professional way of achieving it.

Just over thirty years ago the Cryonics Institute was founded in the USA. Cryonics means suspended animation. The idea quite simply is when you die the blood is pumped out of you and the body is then frozen slowly and stored in liquid nitrogen at −196°C. There are other innovations but without going into too much detail that is virtually it. For those who might wish to avail themselves of this service in our country a London funeral director, Barry Albin-Dyer, has become the European agent for the Cryonics Institute in Detroit. The cost at the time of writing I understand is £17,500 each. Mr Albin-Dyer begins the preparation here and then you are flown off to Detroit where there are the only facilities for deep-freeze and storage. The process is completed and there you will remain until a cure is discovered for the cause of your demise and at the same time a way is found to revive you.

Sounds a bit like *Sleeping Beauty*; I think I prefer the Disney version.

Incidentally it is rumoured that Walt Disney has been a recipient of the deep-freeze and that the singer Michael Jackson and film director Woody Allen have shown interest in the process. Allen was once said to have remarked, 'I don't want to live on in my work, I want to live on in my apartment.'

Some scientists, however, throw a damper on the whole idea. Dr Neil Henderson at the Institute of Cryogenics at Southampton University points out that cryogenics is the very real science of investigating the use of very low temperatures in industry and describes 'cryonics' as science fiction. Dr David Pegg, who specialises in low temperature biology at the University of York, states that what these people are attempting has no scientific basis. It is comparatively simple to freeze a body; the real trick is defrosting and reviving them. He goes on to say that no one has ever successfully frozen a complete organ to date without it sustaining damage. Up to now it has only been possible to freeze certain cells and they have all been healthy ones.

Of course, religious bodies, if you will excuse the pun, do not approve of cryonics. As far as Christians are concerned it completely contradicts their teaching. When you die it is either heaven or hell, and I understand that even hell is probably not an option now. The real problem is the soul. When we die the soul goes to heaven – or so we believers fervently hope. If we then freeze the body it must become soulless. If at some time in the future it is revived successfully, you have a body but no soul. My own personal view is that one life down here is probably enough and I am very happy to settle for heaven if they will have me. After all I am certain to know more people up there, I think. If I was revived say a hundred years from now and reinstated I would not know anyone and the world might not even with all its faults be as agreeable as I think it is today. Just one final thought: after spending all those years in the USA, would I have to reapply for British citizenship?

Something that has caused concern in many areas of our country is the shortage of burial ground. The fact that we are such a small country must be one of the main reasons. Many cities and towns have cemeteries many that have been in existence for one hundred years and much longer and were located on the boundary, as it was then, of the city or town. As these cities and towns have evolved over the years the cemeteries end up being left in the middle encircled by houses or other developments. When they become full and there is no additional land to expand to, you then have a big problem.

Churchyards in villages face the same predicament as the cemeteries. New housing has probably surrounded the church; some churches have managed to acquire land adjacent to the churchyard and others have managed to buy alternative sites on the edge of their village, but for those that have not there is the same dilemma. Strange as it may seem cremation is probably one of the main contributory factors to the problem; 70 per cent of funerals in this country involve cremation. Up until the 1950s burial was preferred.

During the next thirty years many new crematoriums were opened throughout the country, the first being at Woking in 1885. There are now two hundred and thirty. This was accompanied by a quite dramatic move from burial to cremation. A consequence of this was to ease the pressure on the cemeteries and churchyards. If this trend had not occurred they would have been looking for land much sooner. Some of the local authorities may have been guilty of taking the view that everyone would eventually turn to cremation, but that will never happen. Someone once said this to my father and his reply was, 'You will never ever be able to tell people what kind of funeral they may have.'

Let's take York, for instance. The original burial grounds for the city were the churchyards within the city wall and there were very many churches. If you visit the churches today you can see that some of the churchyards remain but they have not been used since 1855. In 1837, the year of Queen Victoria's accession, some leading citizens decided that York required a cemetery of its own and the York Public Cemetery Company was founded. This was not without considerable opposition, mainly from the churches, who saw it as a threat to their income. They and others also thought it was not a very honourable practice to make money exclusively from people dying and some members of the public thought the new land was too far from the city.

The eight acre site was beyond the southern boundary of York about half a mile from the city centre. James Piggot Pritchett, the architect who designed Huddersfield railway station and co-designed the York Minster Song School, was commissioned to design and build a cemetery chapel. This also did not please the clergy, as it was providing an alternative venue for a funeral service; but the venture went ahead.

The York Public Cemetery Company continued to acquire land until 1938. By that time it had grown to twenty-four acres, its present size. It had its own stone yard and showroom and was doing a thriving business selling memorials. The Company had a virtual monopoly, except for the Quaker burial ground on Heslington Road, until 1915, when a new cemetery was opened by the parish council at Fulford, a village three miles to the south of York. I presume it was originally intended for Fulford residents, but over the years it became an alternative burial place for those residents in York who for whatever reason did not like York Cemetery. Yet the vast majority of burials were still taking place at the old cemetery. In 1945 the name was changed to The York Cemetery Company and it became a limited liability company.

The cemetery was profitable until the 1950s, although the directors knew the writing was on the wall long before that. The income from the memorials and new graves had been gradually decreasing and by this time they had simply run out of land. In 1966, the York Cemetery Company went into voluntary liquidation and a liquidator was appointed. The cemetery had to remain open because people had rights of burial to existing graves but there was very little money. The cemetery began to deteriorate and became overgrown and the cemetery chapel fell into disrepair. It limped on until 1979 when the liquidator left and the company was dissolved. In 1984, the roof of the cemetery chapel collapsed and that same year a steering group, the Friends of York Cemetery, was set up. In 1987, the York Cemetery Trust, who now own and run the cemetery, was formed. Their principal aim was the survival of the cemetery as a viable concern. Their only income was the fees they received for the reopening of existing graves and grave maintenance, as the memorial business had been sold. In time they found areas of land in the cemetery that were unused and started to sell grave spaces again.

In January 1987, Paul Levens was appointed as the first Warden of York Cemetery, and his remit was the implementation and development of the ecological land management plan, plus the supervision of the York Council for Voluntary Service Teams, which began to work on new projects for the cemetery. In addition he was responsible for the funerals in the cemetery. In August, after receiving grants from English Heritage, the Pilgrim Trust, York City Council, the Joseph Rowntree Memorial Trust, the York Civic Trust, the Noel G. Terry Trust and H.B. Raylor

Limited, work began on the restoration of the cemetery Chapel, a Grade 2 listed building. By 1988 the first stage of the restoration was over. The work carried on and the first funeral service was held in the restored chapel in 1991.

The year before, 1990, Bill Shaw was appointed Warden. Bill has introduced exotic and ornamental shrubs and nature trails into the cemetery. There was already an abundance of wildlife. The knock-on effect of this has been that school parties come to the cemetery for educational nature walks, where the guide relates the history of the cemetery and points out the last resting place of some of York's notable citizens. In addition to funeral services being held in the cemetery Chapel, many cultural activities take place there such as exhibitions, concerts and conferences. All this contributes to the income for the Cemetery Trust. Thanks to a lot of people who cared enough and persevered, the old cemetery has had a second chance.

For anyone who would like an in-depth and detailed history of the cemetery, a book called *This Garden of Death*, the history of York Cemetery, written by Hugh Murray, was published in 1991.

York still has not got a municipal cemetery of its own other than Dringhouses, a small cemetery on the southwest boundary of York. Quite a large area of land was set aside in 1927 but only a very small proportion of it was ever used and it has been full for many years. I am not sure why; maybe someone thought that everyone would turn to cremation when York's own crematorium was opened in 1962.

In 1969 an agreement was made between York Corporation and Fulford Parish Council which permitted York citizens to be interred in Fulford Cemetery for the following fifty years. Up until that time anyone other than a Fulford resident who wished to be interred there was charged double fees. After the agreement was made, York residents could be interred there for the same fee as Fulford residents. In return the York Corporation agreed to be responsible for losses incurred in running the cemetery in proportion to the number of York burials. Fulford now acts as York's burial authority and covers a twenty-six acre site. With the proportion of funerals 70 per cent cremation, the cemetery will last well into the future; but what if it then becomes full, say one hundred years from now? Could the story repeat itself and could Fulford suffer the same fate as York Cemetery? Unless I go in for cryonics I am never going to know.

Footnote: as you go through the gate at Fulford Cemetery about one hundred yards ahead on the main path is a plot of land which acts as a roundabout. It is now known as the Fulford Plot for Fulford residents only. I was told many years ago that the Fulford Parish Council intended to build York's first crematorium there although it never came to fruition. If it had, probably the twentieth-century history of York's burials and cremations would have been totally different.

As I have already said, the churchyards suffer the same fate as cemeteries if they have not been able to acquire land for burial. All Saints Church, Huntington, a village three miles north-east of York, used up the last of their burial ground in the 1980s. They were not able to acquire any land, which meant that any Huntington residents who died and wished to be buried had to find an alternative space elsewhere. The neighbouring villages were not too enthusiastic to accommodate them because of their own limited space. This very often meant the only option left was Fulford Cemetery and as Huntington did not come under the York City Council scheme the families had to pay double fees, which was quite a considerable amount. Local councillors from Huntington and two other villages formed the Huntington Burial Board and managed to acquire a 1¼ acre site in New Lane, Huntington, about three-quarters of a mile from the churchyard. After opposition, mainly from residents nearby, the cemetery had its first burial in 1988.

Just a word about the opposition from local residents. I think it is quite understandable that if you are living in a pleasant residential area and then someone decides they want to plonk a cemetery opposite you that you might not think it is a terribly good idea. The residents of New Lane probably thought that funerals would be arriving several times a day. This is not the case; it is possible that there could be two funerals in one day but they could go two or three weeks without one at all.

Funeral directors have the same problem. No one wants to live next to a funeral director and they very often experience great difficulty with planning permission for new premises. However, cemeteries, crematoriums and funeral directors have to go somewhere as the public, whether they like it or not, are going to need them some day. When planning where any of these places are to be situated it is extremely important that the general public, and particularly any people living nearby, are taken into consideration in order that everything that is done is as discreet as possible and certain entrances are camouflaged.

Because of the shortage of burial spaces several private cemeteries or burial grounds have started to appear. The ones that I am personally aware of are situated in rural areas usually far enough away from any residential neighbourhoods so as not to be the targets of any objections.

Several years ago I was contacted by Robert Goodwill, a farmer from Terrington, a village fifteen miles north of York. I already knew Robert, having worked for his family previously. He realised there was a very limited choice for families in the York area who wished for their funeral to be interment. Terrington churchyard had been full for many years. The Terrington Burial Board had acquired an additional piece of land half a mile outside the village. Robert owned a 2½ acre plot of land adjoining this burial ground and decided it was an ideal site for a private cemetery. He asked me to visit Terrington to view the proposed site and give my opinion.

Terrington is a lovely village in the Howardian Hills. Robert's proposed cemetery is down a narrow country lane and has an elevated position overlooking the Vale of York. The only possible drawback was the distance people would have to travel to visit the grave after the funeral. It is probably half an hour from York; but Fulford Cemetery on the edge of the city itself, requires a journey in a car of probably fifteen or twenty minutes – not a lot different if you look at it that way.

Robert obtained planning permission without much trouble. The families have two choices: traditional burials with grave spaces side by side, and woodland burials among trees and shrubs. Everything seemed to be progressing well, when objections to the cemetery were made, mainly from people in Terrington, who feared that the village might become a main thoroughfare for funerals. I won't go into the legal technicalities that followed but the original planning permission was withdrawn and a public enquiry followed. By this time several families had already purchased burial plots. The name of the cemetery is Mowthorpe Garden of Rest. It is a very secluded and peaceful place and there is no doubt in my mind that many families from a far wider area than York would be grateful to have access to such a picturesque cemetery for their final resting place. Anyone from any part of the country could be interred in the Mowthorpe Garden of Rest if they so wished and everyone is charged the same.

I might add here that the first interment at Mowthorpe was in February, 1997, a month before final planning consent was granted in March.

Over the years, but very rarely, someone decides that when they die they would like to be interred in their own garden. Provided certain environmental requirements are met there is no law that says you may not do so. After all, families who live in stately homes and indeed the Royal Family, do it all the time; but there is a world of difference between Frogmore or a mausoleum in private grounds, and a garden behind a semi-detached in Birmingham.

Let us first look at some of the things you must do if you seriously intend to inter someone on private property.

1. Contact the Department of Environment.

2. Inform the local council who have responsibility for the area of the proposed interment.

As far as I am aware there is no legal requirement to inform the police but I think it would be prudent to do so. Someone unknown to you who witnesses the interment could possibly put a completely different interpretation on the proceedings. Similarly, I think it would be wise to inform your immediate neighbours. They might well object and it would be better for the matter to be resolved at the onset. My understanding is that a minister of religion cannot consecrate or dedicate the ground, but can bless it. You require a bishop to dedicate the ground and an archbishop to consecrate the ground, and these gentlemen are a bit thin on the ground if you will excuse the metaphor.

After the burial has taken place a document recording the interment must be placed with the deeds of the property. If in the future you plan a second interment that might be viewed as starting your own private burial ground and could create difficulties.

One final consideration: when someone has been interred in a private garden, any house move in the future is not going to be easy. In fact before the interment has taken place I expect you have to be fairly certain that you are going to remain in that house for life. It is extremely unlikely that anyone other than a relation of your own family would want to purchase a house with a member of your family buried in the garden. The alternative is of course to take them with you and that means exhumation, accompanied by all the legal requirements, and surely under these circumstances there must be a certain amount of stress involved. I am not saying you should not bury someone in your garden if that is what you and your family really want; but you must surely consider all the implications before making such a decision.

Something that is always going to be controversial is disturbing existing burial grounds. Of course, as I have said earlier, single exhumations take place for many reasons; but mass exhumation is a different matter. The Necropolis Company came into being by a private act of parliament in 1852 and is empowered to exhume and re-inter human remains. They have vast experience of this very delicate task. Most of us would quite naturally think that burial grounds may not be disturbed but that is not so. Yet if they are, there is always justification for it; maybe the burial ground has deteriorated to such an extent that it has become a health hazard, or a church is demolished in a city centre and all that remains is a very old churchyard. The occupants are exhumed and re-interred elsewhere with dignity.

Many years ago I remember my father telling me of a church situated on cliffs on the Yorkshire coast with its churchyard extending to the edge of the cliff top. Gradually over the years there had been cliff erosion and some of the graves and their contents had disappeared into the sea. Obviously when an event like that occurs something must be done. Other instances where large scale exhumation has been required are for new roads or road extensions. In all these cases legal and religious requirements must be taken into consideration. The laws that must be referred to are:

1. Disused Burial Grounds (Amendment) Act, 1981.

2. The Town and Country Planning Act.

3. Bishop's Faculties.

4. Home Office Licences.

5. Church of England Pastoral Measure.

6. Private Acts of Parliament.

7. Various other religious laws.

Another matter that is going to promote controversy is the proposed reuse of burial grounds or cemeteries for re-interment. There are two sets of circumstances where this might occur.

Firstly, where an interment takes place on ground where burials have previously taken place; this was common practice in London in the seventeenth and eighteenth centuries and involved disturbing existing human remains by actually digging through them. I have no knowledge that this takes place anywhere now, and thankfully is technically illegal; but what some cemeteries and burial grounds are considering is exhuming the remains in very old graves, placing them in containers of some sort, then digging the graves to a greater depth and re-interring them, then reusing the graves. I understand that this proposal would require an act of parliament. It would also need the forbearance and understanding of a great number of people.

The second method used in London and some other cities requires quantities of soil to be brought into the cemetery to raise the existing ground level. This enables additional interments to take place. I understand that this is something referred to as double-deck burial grounds. There are some cemeteries where this method has been used more than once, resulting in a considerable increase to the original height of the land.

These might seem to be fairly drastic measures to enable the continuing use of a cemetery, but what the councils, private owners and burial boards are trying to do to the best of their ability is to keep the cemetery in use as long as they can. For a family to be told that there is no more room in a cemetery where maybe several generations of their relations have been interred can be extremely distressing. I do not pretend to know what the long-term solution might be, but anyone who is prepared to open a new cemetery or burial ground in a place where no offence will be caused to others, and where at the same time its legal and financial future is properly secured, should not be discouraged.

In 1988 I had three weeks' touring holiday in the USA and this included two days in Washington. While there I visited Arlington Cemetery where some of America's most famous people and many war heroes are buried. The story behind how Arlington became America's most famous cemetery is quite extraordinary.

In the centre of the cemetery stands an elegant mansion which, prior to the American Civil War of 1861–1865, was the home of Robert E. Lee. the US army general. On the outbreak of hostilities he joined the Confederate army of the southern states and was subsequently military adviser to Jefferson Davis, President of the Confederacy. He was famous for his defence of Richmond, Virginia – the

Confederate capital – but was finally defeated at Gettysburg and surrendered to General Grant in April, 1865, at Appomattox Courthouse. After the war President Lincoln was asked what should become of General Lee's mansion and estate. I am not sure of his exact response but I understand it was something on the lines of, 'It's his if he wants it,' However, as you may have gathered, Arlington had been experiencing quite a dramatic transformation during the course of the war. The Union army had begun to inter some of the many thousands of casualties sustained in that very sad conflict on General Lee's estate, and when the war ended in 1865 the mansion was surrounded by very many graves of their brave and unfortunate fallen soldiers. Whose idea it was to convert the general's backyard into a graveyard I do not know. Could it have been old Abe? General Lee never returned to Arlington, not even when he died five years later in 1870. He is buried in the chapel grounds at the Washington and Lee University at Lexington, Virginia.

Several years ago I was approached by the Macmillan nurse tutor responsible for the vocational and professional studies at the North Yorkshire College of Health Studies and was asked if I would be prepared to give a talk to a group of nurses as part of their course on the continuing care of the dying patient and the family. I agreed and they came to my premises shortly afterwards. This became the forerunner of many other subsequent talks I gave to student nurses.

The nurses' visits to my premises were in two parts. Firstly I would talk to them about aspects of my profession I thought were relevant to their own careers and then invite them to ask questions. Then one of my funeral directors would take them on a tour of the premises so that they could see exactly what we did, but in particular what happens to the deceased when they are removed to the chapel from a hospital, nursing home or indeed a private residence. In fact this was the most important part of the visit. When a nurse has been caring for a patient, especially over an extended period, as I am sure you are aware quite a close relationship can build up. If and when that person dies, very often the nurse is asked by the family, 'What happens now?' If the nurses have first-hand knowledge of the funeral director, his premises and his procedures, they are going to be better equipped to respond.

Their visits have now extended into open evenings on a regular basis and are very successful. Not only do students attend but qualified nurses as well.

Over recent years I have given other talks, sometimes they are referred to as lectures to many other groups associated with my profession including trainee funeral directors, clergy and bereavement counsellors.

Quite recently I was invited by the headmaster of a local high school to talk to a group of his pupils about my profession as part of a project they were involved with. It turned out to be one of the most enjoyable and rewarding talks I have given. After I gave the talk I invited questions. This was the first time I had talked to children in these circumstances. I soon discovered that children are completely uninhibited when it comes to asking questions, even on such a sensitive subject as death, and I thoroughly enjoyed the experience. Shortly after my visit I received an envelope from the school containing letters from the children I had talked to thanking me for my visit. They went on to ask me further questions that had not been asked at my visit, or wanted further clarification on some of the things I had talked about.

Naturally, I responded. I would quite happily return to their school at any time, or any other school for that matter. I really felt it had been worthwhile. My grandfather on my mother's side was a school headmaster and I am sure he was aware that I had not been an outstanding scholar; so I think he would have been quite amused that I had assisted in children's education, if only in some small way, in my later years.

In addition, I am invited to give talks to Round Table, Rotary and Women's Institutes. I have never volunteered to speak anywhere because, given my profession, I am not absolutely sure everyone wants to listen; but if invited I will talk to anyone.

Recently we were contacted by a family whom we had previously worked for and asked if we would convey their much loved dog, which had died, to the pet crematorium. Until then I was not even aware there was such a place. Now I do not know whether any of my colleagues might not have approved. We felt there was no way we could decline this request and in due course we conveyed the dog to the pet crematorium which was about thirty miles away. The crematorium is not unlike a conventional crematorium with a reception area and lounge. It is the family's own choice whether they go to the crematorium or someone goes in their place, and if they so wish the crematorium staff are quite prepared to collect the pet themselves.

Not only are the obvious pets such as dogs and cats cremated. No animal, from a horse to a hamster, is a problem. Pets that have been put to sleep from veterinary practices also come in on a regular basis. After the cremation if the family so wish they can have the cremated remains returned to them in a casket or alternatively they can be strewn at the crematorium.

That of course poses the same question as that which is asked at a conventional crematorium: how do I know they are the correct remains? All crematoriums, whether conventional or for pets, take pride in their procedures to make absolutely sure there is no error.

It is not everyone who wants to bury their much loved pet in the back garden; they might not like that idea, plus the same problem can arise as when you bury a relative in your garden: what happens if you decide to move house? Do you leave them there or take them with you? In my view the pets' crematorium provides an excellent alternative.

Just by way of a footnote to crematoriums, a South African engineer, Chris Bellingan, has invented the world's first portable cremation incinerator. He demonstrated it recently at a funeral show in South Africa. It is capable of taking five bodies each time and is environmentally friendly. Other than that I do not know much more about it. I expect it is handy if your local crematorium burns down. Presumably you wheel it along, plug it in and there you go.

Occasionally, someone leaves instructions that when they die they want a traditional horse-drawn funeral. There are several firms in the country who can supply this service and one firm that I have personal knowledge of is Gibsons Carriage Masters. They are members of the National Association of Funeral Directors and have an extensive range of genuine Victorian hearses and mourners' conveyances, quality funeral harness and plumes. Their horses are probably the finest in the country. They are correct carriage horses, described in antique literature as perfect blacks; all are black pure Friesian. You can choose what combination you like, six, four or pairs, and the coaches are driven by Victorian attired professional coachmen. If requested they can also supply white horses and harness.

In this, as in everything else associated to our profession, reliability is paramount. If I had arranged a funeral and promised to supply horses and coaches and then they did not arrive I think I would probably leave the country. This will not happen with Gibsons; they have two bases in Cambridgeshire and Lancashire respectively and will travel anywhere in the UK at short notice, regardless of what time of day the funeral is to take place. They will be there early in the morning along with their own transporter and are thoroughly professional to the extent that they will do a complete dry run of the entire route to ensure there are no hazards which could impede the cortège. Obviously, depending on what horses and carriages the family select determines the cost. Gibsons readily admit that they are not the cheapest available but everything – horses, carriages, harness and personal dress – is of the highest quality, and of course for such an important occasion, reliability. Horse-drawn funerals are a perfect example of how funeral directors are able to turn the clock back so as to arrange and conduct a funeral as it would have been a hundred years ago.

As a complete contrast we have on our staff at J. Rymer a lady who has the title of Liaison Care Officer. As I write she is the latest innovation in our profession. Her role is quite simply to offer help and advice to any bereaved person who feels they might benefit through it. There is complete confidentiality and no charge. There is no set procedure but it will probably follow the following pattern.

During the course of making the arrangements, it is quite possible that the funeral director will detect some anxiety in the person he is arranging things with about something that is not connected with the funeral. For example, perhaps the person who has died has been totally responsible for withdrawing money from the bank and the settlement of accounts. If the person left has no experience whatsoever of money matters, on top of the bereavement the new responsibility can be quite daunting. The funeral director might then at that stage tactfully ask if they would like some help. If they agree the funeral director will inform the liaison care officer who will then make contact. If there is no family, things like cooking a meal to someone who has never attempted it before can be quite a task. If the liaison care officer cannot help herself she will contact someone who can, anyone from Age Concern to Meals on Wheels.

The liaison care officer is not a bereavement counsellor but will listen and help before the funeral and after. She is very often required following a sudden death where no one has been prepared for a dramatic and unexpected change of circumstances. Other areas where she might be of some help are on the day of the funeral. The family might not be happy to leave the house unattended while they are at the funeral, so the liaison care officer will try to arrange for someone to be there during the period of the funeral service. There could be a child or baby that may require minding; the liaison care officer will make every effort to find a place at a crèche for the duration of the funeral.

Finally, after the funeral has taken place and because of the stress at that time, the family very often do not remember everything that was discussed and decided upon whilst making the funeral arrangements, yet feel reluctant to contact the funeral director. Again the liaison care officer is the obvious person to clarify any of this information with the funeral director on a follow-up visit to the family.

Many people are able to go through this period with the help of family and friends, but regrettably some people do not have family or friends, or for various reasons cannot or will not accept their help. Such people often find it much easier to accept assistance from someone they do not know personally.

Recently, Britain's first funeral supermarket opened. I believe the idea originated in France; I expect it is an extension of DIY funerals. I understand it has everything from coffins to memorials. You arrive, collect your trolley and make your selection, although there will have to be a special arrangement to transport the memorial as they can weigh anything from twenty to forty stones. I think I can safely say that only a minority of the public would wish to go through such a procedure and not many funeral directors are going to lose much sleep over it. The bottom line, as always with our profession, is that people must be free to choose the manner in which a funeral is arranged and conducted, regardless of what anyone else might think.

In July, 1945, the Labour Party won the general election by a landslide and Clement Attlee became Prime Minister. They were returned to power in 1950 with a greatly reduced majority and defeated in 1951. During its tenure they introduced a wide-ranging programme of nationalisation and an entire new system of social services. One day through the post my father received notification that the charges he was currently making for funeral arrangements must remain as they were until further notice. Were the government planning the nationalisation of funeral directors? If not, it was certainly a form of state control.

For whatever reason I do not know, but nationalisation never materialised. Maybe they had too much on their plates – or could it have been the realisation by the 'let's nationalise everything that moves' team of what an unmitigated disaster it would have been. It certainly put the wind up my father for a while, along with many others in the profession. Without going into much detail, one thing for sure that would have happened would have been a rapid decline in the service the public received.

In my view, private enterprise is synonymous with service and efficiency: I expect the nearest we got to it again was in the early 1980s when some local councils had the concept of a 'Municipal Funeral Service'. This would take the form of a local authority owning the property and facilities, e.g. hearses and limousines and employing their own funeral directors and staff. As far as I am aware, not one Municipal Funeral Service came into fruition, they were all watered down into 'Tendered Funeral Services' with the councils inviting tenders from local funeral directors.

As far back as 1985, Southwark Council had envisaged that a subsidy of £70,000 per annum would be required for the service, so there was the first obstacle. The second one was the question of legality. The Tendered Funeral Service was a much more attractive proposition. The cost to the local authority would be negligible and there seemed to be no doubts about the legality of the service. Funeral directors, some of them members of the National Association of Funeral Directors, tendered for the work. Those who were successful provided what only could be described as a contract service. The NAFD members are all bound by a code of practice regardless of who they work for, so there could be no cutting of corners and lowering of standards. So you therefore have to assume that the contract service funerals are being subsidised by the company's private funerals. As the tendered price is going to be considerably lower, you might well ask why a funeral director would find it necessary to tender, because in some areas he could not be absolutely sure how many of his existing customers might be tempted to take advantage of a cheaper funeral, although many would never do so, regardless of their circumstances.

One thing that puzzled me about the contract service was presumably the family must have authorisation from the council to go ahead and make the funeral arrangements; a permit or just a slip of paper. What happens if the person dies when the council offices are closed, say at Easter or Christmas? Or in an even worse scenario, they die at home? Does that person have to remain there until the council office reopens and authorisation for a removal is given? If the death occurred at night and you had to wait till next morning it could be bad enough. But suppose the death occurred on the Thursday night before Easter – you could be waiting until the following Tuesday for help.

The private funeral director has to give a 24-hour, 365 days a year service, paying wages to quality trained staff who provide this service, and at the same time he must abide by the principles of the code of practice; none of this can be done on the cheap.

As far as I am aware there are no figures available as to the percentage of people who take advantage of the Tendered Funeral Service, but 10 per cent of all funerals are funded by payments from the Social Fund to people who qualify for assistance.

I mentioned there the code of practice; this is the National Association of Funeral Directors' code. It has had a code of conduct since 1907 but in 1979 a new code of practice was drawn up and agreed with the Office of Fair Trading. Subsequently in 1994 certain amendments were made. These were fundamental changes which demanded more stringent control over principles in the code to give an even higher level of service to the public. Although the present day code is much changed from the 1907 code of conduct it still contains many of the original principles. The present day code covers quality of service, charges and accounts, professional conduct, advertising standards and client confidentiality.

In addition the NAFD has a conciliation service for complaints through the Chartered Institute of Arbitrators and Independent Arbitration Service which hopefully would be able to resolve any dispute. All surveys, including Office of Fair Trading surveys, show that there are very few complaints; but sometimes something goes wrong. Most of these complaints would be resolved with the funeral director concerned. If that failed it would be referred to the NAFD's conciliation service and finally the Chartered Institute of Arbitrators. All professions require a code of practice but to funeral directors, whose work is of such a personal and sensitive nature, it is essential.

When I came into the profession we were making all our own coffins. In fact a very large proportion of our working week was taken up with the construction of coffins. Even if we did not require them for current funerals we would try to make them for stock. If on the very rare occasion we managed to make twelve, which was the maximum we had storage room for at that time, we thought we had done very well.

In the mid-Fifties we were using English elm coffins for our standard funeral. Our middle range was chestnut and for those families who wanted the very best it was oak. The majority of the coffins were polished dark; the others wax polished light. Towards the end of the Sixties the English elm began to decline in quality and our timber merchant suppliers decided to import West African hardwoods such as agba, utile and obeche. Utile was particularly useful to us because it was a mahogany colour and enabled us to continue producing dark polished coffins. We were also having difficulty obtaining good quality English oak. This was not so serious because we used a considerably smaller quantity and we were able to supplement our stock by using Japanese oak and, to a lesser extent, American oak.

We had already begun to make coffins for some of the funeral directors whom we already supplied with hearses and limousines, so even more working hours were required in the workshop. Then in 1963, Clifford Morris, a freelance agent for various manufacturers who supplied to the funeral profession, called at our business on one of his regular visits. Clifford and my father were quite friendly and I used to sit in the office with them if I was able. Clifford told my father he had acquired a new agency and he now was able to supply ready-made coffins. If it had been anyone other than Clifford I think the conversation would have ended there and then as my father thought it strictly taboo for a funeral director to do any other than make his own coffins, but he let him continue and in due course Clifford produced photographs of the coffins. I never discovered whether it was deliberate or not but the coffins were dark polished and looked identical to the ones we were making and supplying ourselves as our standard coffin. If they had been light coloured it might not have worked but with great skill he persuaded my father to purchase twelve coffins. I could not believe my father's reluctance; to me it seemed the obvious thing to do. The price was reasonable and the hours in the workshop would be cut quite dramatically. My father must have been reading my mind, as he turned to me and said, 'Don't think this is how it is going to be.'

I nodded my head in agreement but said to myself, Oh yes it is!

I have talked to various people connected with present day coffin manufacturing including David Fisher, Managing Director of Carrwood in Yorkshire, and Fred Leighton of L.T. and R. Vowles of Upton upon Severn, Worcestershire, and we have found it hard to pinpoint the business in this country which was the first to manufacture and sell coffins rather than timber sets to funeral directors. Fred Leighton tells me that Nicholsons Timber Merchants of Windermere were selling solid elm coffins between 1950 and 1955. Ingalls of Birmingham, who had depots in London, Liverpool, Manchester, Bristol, Leeds and Glasgow, were involved at this time and probably Dottridge Brothers of London. I must apologise if there was a firm selling coffins before them but I am not aware of it.

In time most of the timber merchants who supplied coffin sets to funeral directors started to manufacture and sell complete coffins. I am certainly not right about everything, but I was about us buying coffins; my father soon realised how much easier it was going to be if we purchased coffins rather than making them ourselves and every year we bought an increasing number. We arrived at a point where the only coffins we made ourselves were the specials such as solid oaks. In time we became agents for Ingalls and Dottridge Brothers and stocked coffins for many funeral directors in our area. As new manufacturers came on the scene we would buy from them mainly to compare their products.

Around about 1964 we started to use our first veneered coffins; gradually the only solid coffins we supplied were oak, by this time mainly Japanese oak. We had experimented with veneered coffin sets on inferior solid timbers some years earlier but without much success. As we made the coffins the veneer would chip away and it proved hard to repair. These veneered coffins we were using now were veneered on high density chipboard, professionally manufactured and very often looked better than the real thing.

I have mentioned earlier that I had become a quite competent coffin polisher. With the advent of purchasing coffins, however, I had hardly done any at all. Occasionally we would arrange a funeral, maybe for a family that we had worked for for generations, and they would request that we polish the coffin ourselves in our workshop. By the mid-1980s we had ceased to make any coffins at all and were now purchasing solid oak coffins as well, but we also kept in stock several coffins 'in the white' (unpolished) so we were able to polish them ourselves if called upon. By the 1980s there was only myself left who could polish a coffin. My father had retired and there had seemed little point in teaching my sons and current staff to polish. The consequence of this was if a coffin did require polishing I had to repair to the workshop.

In preparation the coffin needed considerable sandpapering then three coats of polish, two coats of button polish and finished off with one coat of shellac varnish. I think the whole process, which lasted about four hours, must have had novelty value because the staff – full- and part-time, plus any visiting funeral directors – would find their way into the workshop to witness me adorned in a smock, brush in hand, polishing one of the last coffins for J. Rymer. I think the last one I polished was about 1990.

Coffin manufacturers today produce a wide range, not only of coffins but caskets; caskets are widely used in the USA and many other countries, the main difference is they are rectangular instead of the traditional coffin shape.

Those families wanting a so-called 'green' funeral may require a cardboard biodegradable coffin. I personally do not think they are very dignified and the only one I saw was inclined to sag. Not many families want to use these but the old professional funeral director's adage must apply again: if that is what a family really want, we must not stand in their way. I am not totally convinced how much 'greener' these cardboard coffins are. It is a fact that many solid timber coffins are still used, as is solid timber furniture; but a vast quantity of the standard coffins are veneered on chipboard, which is made of cuttings from timber, and cardboard coffins are just wood pulp. It's maybe a case of you can't see the wood for the trees!

Chapter Sixteen

Humour and funerals might seem strange bedfellows but as far as our country is concerned they have in my own experience intermingled on numerous occasions. Whether similar incidents happen in other countries which might raise a smile at a funeral I do not know, but I am sure we have all seen on television how very differently funerals are carried out in some other countries, with scenes of mass hysteria preceding the burial or cremation. It is hard to imagine any humour at all under these circumstances. In fact if some of the incidents I am about to relate had occurred then, they would most likely have increased the frenzy.

Let me say straight away there is nothing funny about a funeral. Indeed as I have recalled earlier some deaths occur in such tragic circumstances that I have never ceased to be amazed how families manage to cope. Nevertheless humorous things do happen and it is not only the funeral director and his staff who are amused, but of course they must not show it, but families smile as well. This is not disrespect but a natural reaction by the British along with their sense of humour and I am sure it helps to relieve tension. In addition many things which are humorous happen that the family are not aware of. I would like to describe some of these as well.

I first became aware that people could laugh at a funeral very soon after I joined the business. We were on our way from York to Harrogate crematorium. I was seated next to the driver in the family's limousine immediately following the hearse. All of a sudden the car began to swerve about and it became clear that we had a puncture. We managed to signal the hearse and pulled into the side of the road. I think we had six passengers in the back – quite a considerable weight. By the time we had stopped the car had a noticeable list. The funeral director (not my father) had to ask the family if they would mind stepping out of the car while the wheel was changed. They thought the whole thing was hilarious and I heard them remark that their father, whose funeral it was, would have thought it so. Now this in itself might not sound particularly amusing but I was quite young then and I think I expected a reaction of annoyance, not amusement. This was my first experience of people actually laughing at a funeral. It was not disrespect, just a natural reaction. Like many incidents in life, at the time they are not funny but then on reflection when you recall the event it can be amusing.

In my father's early days as a funeral director he was called to a house about three streets from our business, maybe five minutes walk away. As he understood it someone had died there. Since there was no chapels of rest in those days, if a person died at home they had to remain at the house until the day of the funeral. It was also common practice to take a board along to the house so the body could be placed on it to keep it straight until a coffin could be made. When my father arrived at the house he was invited inside, board and all. During a short conversation the people there thanked him for coming and invited him to go upstairs, which he did accompanied by two members of the family. They went into a dimly lit bedroom where a gentleman was laid on a bed.

'How long do you think he will last, Mr Rymer?' someone asked.

'Sorry, what did you say?' my father said.

'The doctor thinks he won't make it through the night,' came the reply.

My father was just grateful that the person whose imminent demise they were discussing did not join in the conversation and was hopefully oblivious to it. Without giving a second opinion, my father hurried downstairs, collected his board and beat a hasty retreat.

Another similar incident happened to my father some years later. It was not quite as bad as the one I have just recounted. A man whom my father had known all his life and lived only a few doors from him was very ill. Everyone knew that he was unlikely to recover. One day his son called to see my father with a request from his father for him to visit. Two or three days later my father plucked up courage and went to see him. He knocked on the door and the familiar voice of Fred called, 'Come in, Jack.' His bed had been brought downstairs and was in the corner of the living room. They carried out a normal conversation at first, as they had always done when they met, then he said to my father 'Where do you think I will look best, Jack, here or under the window?'

He was of course referring to the position of his coffin. My father did not know how to respond; he just smiled and got up to leave. As he was going through the door Fred shouted after him, 'If I see your old feller I'll tell him you're doing all right.' This was a reference to my grandfather, whom Fred had known quite well, and his anticipated reunion with him in the not too distant future. I would like to think that reunion did take place. If so, it was just a little less than two weeks after my father's visit.

If there is one thing that can improve a funeral it is the weather. If it is a bright sunny day it can really help; if there's no sun, it's raining or snowing, it just contributes to a miserable atmosphere. Worse still is fog. One winter morning not long after I joined the business we had a funeral service in church very early one morning. The previous night had been dreadful, cold with thick freezing fog. The morning showed very little improvement. After the service we made our way very slowly even for a cortège to York Cemetery where the interment was to take place. It was hard to imagine a worse day for a funeral. We removed the coffin from the hearse and started our long walk to the grave where, in this very old twenty-four acre cemetery, you could hardly see a hand in front of you. There are maybe five long paths which run the complete length of the cemetery. Off these paths must run literally hundreds of smaller paths, in other words a maze. Very often even in good light you were not able to see the grave until you were a few yards from it.

As we proceeded into the cemetery we were following the priest, my father, and George Jackson, the foreman at York Cemetery, who always guided us to the place of interment. People said that George knew every grave in the cemetery and I think they were probably right. I was a bearer at the front of the coffin along side Syd Walker who had worked for us for many years and was quite a character. We were talking, which I expect we should not have been doing. Syd was explaining something to me that had happened the previous night. My head was down as I was trying to hear what Syd was saying. When I looked up, the priest, George and my father had disappeared. They had obviously turned off on one of the smaller paths and we had kept on walking on the main path.

'What are we going to do now, Syd?' I whispered.

'Keep walking, they will find us,' he answered.

After what seemed an age the figure of George Jackson began to loom out of the fog stood at the end of one of the many paths. He just shook his head and smiled. We turned right and right again and very soon arrived at the grave. George might have been smiling but my father was not. I do not think the family were even aware of the detour so all was well.

Of course one of the dubious privileges of being young is you are the most likely candidate to get the blame, and I did.

Cemeteries, burial grounds and churchyards are places where sometimes things go wrong. Very often that can mean humour as well. Digging graves requires a certain degree of skill and the funeral director has to have complete trust in the gravedigger. Firstly, that a new grave has been dug in the correct place. Secondly, if it is an existing grave that the correct one has been reopened. Most cemeteries have plans, as do churchyards and burial grounds; regrettably sometimes they are incomplete and extreme care and diligence are required in order to locate the correct grave.

Depending on the texture of the soil a grave sometimes requires shoring up to prevent collapse. On several occasions a grave has collapsed and had to be re-dug and on more than one occasion this has happened while the service is taking place in church. Then, frantic efforts by the gravedigger are required to have the grave ready in time for the committal service and interment.

On one such occasion we had a lot of trouble with the grave. When we finally arrived at the graveside for the interment we were extremely relieved when the coffin had been safely lowered into the ground and made sure the mourners did not stand too close to the edge of the grave. The minister was about halfway through the committal service when the ground on which he was stood gave way and he slid gracefully into the grave and ended up sitting on the coffin. The most remarkable thing was he still had the prayer book in his hand. Fortunately, the grave was not very deep and we soon had him out. Thankfully he was not hurt but his surplice was covered in mud. He apologised to the family, for what I do not know, and continued the service as if nothing had happened.

After the service the family made their way back to the cars. Whilst they were walking back myself and the other bearers were carrying the remainder of the flowers to the graveside. By the time I got back to the car the minister had gone. The main family mourners though were literally propped up against the limousine convulsed in laughter. It took several minutes before we were able to persuade them to get into the car for the return journey.

Sometimes we have a funeral and the interment is to take place at a burial ground or churchyard where there is no gravedigger. If this is so it is always the responsibility of the funeral director to get the grave dug. One cold winter week I had to arrange such a funeral. The service was to take place in York and the interment at a very old burial ground about ten miles outside the city. The Clerk to the Council who was responsible for the burial ground informed me that he did not have a gravedigger and I would have to provide my own. Normally this would not be a problem as most funeral directors have one or two freelance gravediggers they can call on. Owing to various circumstances, including illness, I could not get a gravedigger.

In desperation I turned to Harry Cook, who I have mentioned earlier. Harry had done most things in our profession while working for us, including digging the occasional grave but he was no longer a young man and I was reluctant to ask him. However, Harry knew I was in a spot and agreed to dig the grave. What made things worse was that we were extremely busy that week and there were numerous other things Harry could have been doing. The one thing Harry did not do was drive so I had to take him to the burial ground along with the spade and other equipment. It was a bitterly cold day and the burial ground was in a very exposed place. To make matters worse it was sleeting with a cold wind. I asked Harry how long it would take him to dig the grave so I knew what time to return. He said, 'Give me two and a half to three hours.' I thanked him again for helping me out, went to the car and returned to York.

For some reason I cannot recall my father was not there that week. As the day progressed we became busier and busier and I was unable to leave the office. Instead of returning for Harry at about 11.30 a.m. it was gone 2 p.m. when I eventually returned. As I approached the burial ground Harry was nowhere to be seen. I got out of the car and walked up the path and eventually to the grave. Still no Harry. I called out his name and heard this voice I knew so well whimper, 'I'm here, you bugger.'

Harry had squatted down behind the largest headstone he could find to shelter from the bitter cold and was not happy with me. I apologised profusely and helped him to his feet. His legs were that cold he could hardly walk and I had to help him back to the car. Then I went back and collected the spade and the rest of the equipment. Harry always wore a trilby hat and when I got back in the car I immediately noticed he had not got it on.

'Where is your hat, Harry?' I asked.

'A bloody cow's eaten it,' he said shaking his head. 'I put it on the wall whilst I was digging the grave. Next time I looked this bloody big cow was chomping it!'

'I'll buy you a new one,' I said quickly.

'Too bloody right you will,' Harry said as he sat there shivering.

Within ten minutes of leaving the burial ground I saw a roadside pub and although I had by now a strict rule not to drink alcohol during the day I thought this would have to be an exception. I pulled up outside the pub and helped a not yet mobile Harry inside. It was about on closing time but there was still a quite large log fire burning in the bar. I got Harry into a chair as close to the fire as I could, got myself half a bitter and Harry a double whisky. This was followed very quickly by another double and by that time Harry had begun to thaw. I never asked Harry to dig another grave: what with the abuse, double whiskies and new trilby hat, it was too painful and expensive.

Another occasion when we had to provide our own gravedigger always remains clear in my mind. The service was to take place at a village church about twelve miles from York followed by the interment in the churchyard. The rector informed my father that he did not have a gravedigger but suggested we contact a man called Eddie Hick at a village a few miles away. He was not on the telephone and my father dispatched me to find out if he was available and if so negotiate terms. I met Eddie at his house. He agreed to dig the grave. He did not have any transport so I arranged to pick him up next day, take him to the church, then return in the afternoon to take him back home. This I did. On the day of the funeral I collected Eddie again and took him to the church. We were there a good hour before the service so that Eddie could check and prepare the grave for the interment. The funeral went off smoothly.

After the mourners had left the churchyard Eddie began to fill in the grave, with a little help from myself. I had my portable radio with me and was listening to the commentary on the test match. After every burial has taken place there is an excess of soil left which has been displaced by the coffin. If the gravedigger is working in his own cemetery or churchyard he would know how to dispose of it but if you are digging the grave in unfamiliar surroundings it is not so easy. Eventually, Eddie found a place to dispose of the soil but it was a considerable distance from the grave and we decided that a wheelbarrow would come in handy.

Adjacent to the churchyard was a farm and Eddie decided to go and ask them to lend him a wheelbarrow. He had been gone about ten minutes when I heard a shout followed by a barking dog and looked up to see Eddie vaulting this not so low wall, minus a wheelbarrow and a section of his trousers. It seemed that there was only this large dog in residence at the farm and it had not taken kindly to the unexpected visitor. Eddie did not strike me as the most athletic gravedigger I had ever met, and indeed he was no longer a young man, but just for a short period that summer afternoon this most amiable of men became an Olympic hurdler, at the same time expressing un-Cruft's-like comments about the farmer's dog.

While I am talking about incidents in cemeteries and graveyards, I must tell you of something that only occurred a few years ago. We had a funeral service at a York church to be followed by the interment at a local cemetery. When we arrived at the cemetery we removed the coffin, which was quite heavy, from the hearse and proceeded to the graveside. The vicar who had conducted the service was quite a character; he was much liked by many people, including funeral directors and their staff, and renowned for his sense of humour.

When the bearers arrived at the grave they removed the coffin from their shoulders and then just two bearers lowered it on to the battens over the grave, where it remains while the webbing is placed through the handles so it may be lowered into the grave. But as the bearers were bending down, the strain on one of the bearers' trousers became too much and they split, not just a small split but from the waistband to the crotch. What made it worse was the bearer had his back to the vicar who was already in position at the head of the grave ready to conduct the committal service. The parting of the ways had revealed a gaudy pair of underpants. We do not think the family who were stood several yards from the grave were aware of the mishap. The funeral director and the other bearers certainly were; the bearers lowered the coffin into the grave and the three whose trousers were still intact beat a hasty retreat having great difficulty keeping a straight face.

The bearer with the damaged trousers had until now managed to keep his back to the vicar even when lowering the coffin, but somehow he needed to leave the grave without drawing attention to himself.

At this point he whispered to the vicar, 'I've torn my trousers.'

The vicar responded, 'I know you have, please go away please, please go away.'

All the poor man wanted to do was laugh. Of course he could not, he had a service to conclude. The bearer managed to back away from the grave in a manner reminiscent of a Tudor courtier leaving the presence of the first Queen Elizabeth, and somehow the vicar managed to carry on with the service, an accomplishment considering the circumstances above and beyond the call of duty.

Until I started compiling some of the humorous incidents I had not realised that such a great proportion had taken place when the funeral had been interment rather than cremation. I expect the reason must be that they are more likely to occur in cemeteries and churchyards than crematoriums. As I have said earlier, not all the funerals that we were involved with were ones we were directing. We hired our hearses and limousines to other funeral directors as well. On one such occasion we were in cortège making our way to a village church on the outskirts of York for a service in church followed by the interment in the churchyard. I was driving the first limousine following the hearse. The church was situated right on the roadside on a long straight piece of country road. As we approached the church I could see the church quite clearly and a portion of the churchyard at the roadside. I could also see what looked like a man vigorously digging a grave. I thought this cannot be our grave, there must be another funeral at a later date; but then I caught sight of our funeral director in the hearse, whose arms had started to move about in an animated fashion.

All of a sudden I concluded that this was our grave. As the hearse drew up outside the church, the funeral director was out before it had stopped and was making a beeline for the grave. The gravedigger was only about ankle-deep in the grave and obviously had no chance of completing his task before the service was over. Our funeral director told him in no uncertain terms what he thought of his efforts, along with some expletives that I hope the rector had not heard before, as he was now standing at the church door and was in easy hearing distance of the admonishment. Before the funeral service could begin the funeral director and the minister had the thankless task of informing the family of the position. After some discussion it was decided that they would go ahead with the service, leave the coffin in church and return later in the day for the interment.

Afterwards we discovered what had happened. The funeral director had met the gravedigger during the course of making the funeral arrangements, asked him if he would be prepared to dig the grave and he agreed. He also asked him how much he would require in payment. This was something the funeral director would normally do, so that he would be in a position to give the family an estimate of the funeral expenses, but then he made the mistake of paying him. Unfortunately the gravedigger liked a drink, and instead of going to the churchyard he retired to the pub. I expect the moral of this story is, do not pay the digger until you have a hole.

As I have recalled I started out as a pianist, albeit for a short time. I continued playing mainly for myself for quite a number of years and on one occasion it proved useful. My father had arranged a funeral at a village church just outside York. The next day after making the arrangements we received a telephone call from the vicar saying he was sorry but his organist was ill and would be unable to play at the funeral. He did not have a deputy and asked my father if he could provide an organist. Initially my father thought that it would not be a problem but after several enquiries he drew a blank. It was then that he got the bright idea that I could play. I told my father that I was a pianist and I had never played an organ in my life.

'Same thing,' he said, 'you can do it.' My father was also a pianist and he knew it was not the same thing, but he had already informed the family of the predicament and they were upset at the thought that they would not be able to have hymns at the funeral, so I was elected. In order to avoid a complete catastrophe the vicar and my father thought that I should have a dress rehearsal. So it was decided that I would go to the village, meet the vicar at the church and see what I could make out. I cannot remember whether I was driving by then or not; if I was I did not have the use of a car and had to cycle to the village which was several miles from York.

The vicar was waiting for me at the church door. I introduced myself and we went inside. Many ministers are organists or have some basic knowledge of music. This gentleman appeared not to have, or maybe he thought that if he did not get too closely aligned with me, and my performance was a disaster, he might escape some of the fallout. We went down the church to the organ. The vicar switched on a light which illuminated the organ and I gently touched one of the keyboards. Not a sound. The vicar suggested I pull out some of the stops. This I did, and eventually after pulling some out and putting others in I managed to get a sound. The vicar had managed to persuade the family to have just one hymn. I do not think his nerves could have stood two. After my several attempts at playing this hymn, the vicar said that he could nearly recognise it and it would have to do. All I needed now was a piece of music to play as the coffin was being carried into church and for the end of the service when the coffin and family were leaving church. I decided that Handel's *Largo* would be suitable. I also knew the piece reasonably well, which helped.

On the day of the funeral I again had to cycle to the village and arrived there in plenty of time to give myself a bit more practice. When the moment of truth arrived and the coffin began its entry into church I started to play Handel's *Largo* hoping fervently that Georg Friedrich wherever he was did not happen to be listening that day. I did have one thing in my favour: I was completely hidden from everyone's view by a maroon curtain held in place by enormous wooden rings. At least I could not see people's faces. And if things went badly, no one could throw anything at me.

After the bearers had carried the coffin into the church, one of them whispered to my father, 'Who is the ruddy organist?' My father replied that as the coffin was very close to the organist's curtain he should have a look over the top when they collected the coffin at the close of the service.

I managed to play the hymn. The hardest part of this, as it turned out, was keeping count of the verses. A little further on in the service I thought I heard the vicar say to the congregation, 'In a moment we will sing the Twenty-Third Psalm.' I thought there must have been a sudden change to the service. As it happened there was a copy of the Twenty-Third Psalm to Crimmond on the organ which again made me think there had been a change of plan and I had not been informed. Shortly afterwards I heard the vicar mention the Twenty-Third Psalm and I started to play the tune as way of an introduction.

Almost immediately the vicar's head appeared over the curtain. 'We're saying this, not singing it,' he said, with a sarcastic smile. I stopped abruptly and was grateful for the curtain.

As the service came to its conclusion the bearers walked down the church for the coffin. By this time they were all curious to know who was sitting being the curtain. They all had a peek as they lifted the coffin on to their shoulders; finding it difficult no doubt to restrain a smile when they discovered who the culprit was.

The only people who seemed genuinely happy with the performance were the family and I expect that's all that mattered.

One happy footnote was that the vicar insisted that I accept the organist's fee – thirty shillings, or £1.50 today. He probably hoped it was severance pay. It was a lot of money then and it made the whole thing worthwhile. Incidentally, I was never invited again, I cannot think why!

One problem that all funeral directors have is that you can never say to a family, I am sorry but I am very busy this week, come back next week. It is a funeral director's job to have the funeral on the day and time as near as possible to the family's wishes. This sometimes means having to employ additional staff at exceptionally busy periods. Consequently most funeral directors have to have part-time drivers and bearers on the payroll. Very often these are men who are retired or semi-retired. Back in the 1960s we had a period when it was difficult to obtain part-time staff and one week I was that desperate I turned to my oldest friend Roderick Mackenzie ('Mac' to his friends) for help.

Mac worked for his father who was in business in the city – not as a funeral director. He said he was prepared to come as long as his father did not find out. I cannot remember where the funeral took place but the cortège did have to travel through the city. Mac was sitting behind me in the hearse with his hand up along the side of his head trying to obscure his face. Unfortunately for him he was not successful. An eagle-eyed friend of his father spotted him and told him. Whether it had malicious intent or not I do not know, but his father was not pleased and Mac was carpeted, the message being that if Mac wanted to work for Jack Rymer it was fine with him, but it was not going to be in his time. After that Mac was somewhat reluctant to help unless we were desperate but he did again, next time undetected.

Ken Dickinson, a great friend of mine, also helped me once when I was working for the Coroner. We were playing snooker at our club when I received a telephone call from the police to remove a body from a nursing home as soon as possible. The Coroner's Officer was unable to go with me and said he would meet me at the hospital. I tried to contact my staff but could not and because of the urgency needed to move quickly Ken offered to come with me and I gladly accepted. He performed as if he had been doing this job all his life and I was extremely grateful.

A few years ago we had a funeral director called Ron Fairbairn who was a Scot. Ron was articulate and quite at home in anyone's company regardless of their background, an invaluable asset for a funeral director. One day he made funeral arrangements with a family at the office whose aunt had died while on a cruise. As in any profession, when you are dealing with a set of circumstances which happens only rarely you have to read up on the procedure and make additional enquiries. All the formalities and arrangements were completed, Ron met the cruise liner, removed the lady to York and the funeral took place.

Incredibly, within literally a few days I personally received a telephone call from a gentleman whose sister had died during a cruise. He was quite naturally upset, but he seemed irritated as well, which is not uncommon in such circumstances. He explained what had happened and requested that a funeral director should call on him. He went on to say that he did not want anyone to attend unless they were extremely conversant with deaths which occur on cruise liners. Happily passengers do not die on cruise liners every day so there will not be too many funeral directors who would have to obtain information and ask a few questions before embarking on such arrangements (no pun intended).

I called Ron into the office and reported the telephone conversation to him. A smile began to appear on his face. 'I think that might be a job for me,' he said in that purring Scottish accent of his.

Indeed it was; he made an appointment to see the gentleman, who was most impressed with his knowledge and expertise; of course Ron neglected to tell him of his previous arrangements only a few days earlier.

Many humorous incidents that I am aware of concern another firm of funeral directors, Chapman Medd, who are in business in the small market town of Easingwold, fifteen miles from York. As well as Easingwold they arrange and conduct funerals in many of the surrounding villages and have an excellent reputation. They are also well known in the antiques world and have a shop in Easingwold. Nigel Medd arranges and conducts the funerals now. He is the son of Ken Medd who was about twenty years older than me and sadly died in 1980. Ken and I were great friends, socially and in business. He had great knowledge of the profession and helped me on numerous occasions particularly when my father was on holiday. We both possessed the same sense of humour and occasionally played practical jokes on each other.

I first met Ken when he began to hire our hearses and limousines for his funerals. We had just acquired a new fleet and Ken thought they would enhance the quality of his funerals. They now have their own vehicles but in those days we supplied all the vehicles for their funerals. They were far and away our largest customer and there were not many days in the week that we were not involved with their funerals. For many years I drove the hearse myself for Ken. Not only was I looking after our best customer but we enjoyed each other's company, and without loss of dignity or respect there were many times when something humorous occurred.

My first experience of Ken's humour was when I drove the hearse for him on a funeral at Coxwold. This as you may recall was where our family lived before they came to York in 1848. The service was at Coxwold church followed by the interment in the churchyard. The gravedigger for Coxwold church at this time was Bob Featherstone. Ken, Bob and Mrs Featherstone knew each other quite well and apparently whenever Ken had a funeral at Coxwold and he had time he was invited back to Bob and Mrs Featherstone's cottage, which was not far from the church, for a cup of tea. On this day after the funeral Ken invited me back with him. I said I would wait outside in the hearse but he insisted I went in with him. I drew the hearse up outside the cottage and we walked to the door. Ken knocked, opened the door, stepped inside and I followed. As we stood in the doorway Mrs Featherstone emerged from another room. She greeted Ken then asked who I was.

'This is David Rymer,' he told her.

'David who?' she retorted. Ken repeated my name.

'I hope you are no relation to them Rymers who used to live here,' she said.

'Well, actually, yes I am,' I said nervously.

'Get him out, Ken!' she shouted, 'I don't want any of those wicked Rymers in my house – no woman is safe from them.'

My first thought was I'm being set up here but after a further look at Mrs Featherstone's face I was not too sure.

Ken then said, 'It's one hundred and twenty years since they were here, they must have changed.'

'I'm not taking that risk,' she said, shaking her head.

I then glanced at Ken and detected the smallest flicker of a smile and realised I had been set up. By this time Mrs Featherstone was also smiling; it had been a very convincing performance. Bob returned home before we left and enquired how it had gone, saying he wished he had been there. So he had been in on the set-up as well. As we drove away from Coxwold that day I was already planning my revenge.

I have always had the ability to disguise my voice on the telephone and although not making a habit of it have occasionally done it with my friends, sometimes imitating a person they knew or just an anonymous voice. I decided that this was the best way to repay Ken so on more than one occasion I would telephone Ken at his office pretending to make funeral arrangements. I of course made sure he was on his own. I used two accents, one a broad Yorkshire country accent and the other a little more sophisticated. In addition I said I was telephoning from some fictitious address and from an area which Ken would not be totally familiar with. I would start the conversation off in the normal way. Gradually my requirements for the funeral would become increasingly bizarre and Ken's confident professional manner would start to deteriorate. When eventually he discovered it was me, the abuse was something quite unrepeatable but as I pointed out to him, it was first-class experience for him for whenever he received a hoax call or maybe a 'nutcase' telephoning, such as all funeral directors unfortunately receive from time to time.

Most of us are able to detect a call that is not genuine and have certain procedures with which to establish the authenticity of the caller. If we fail to do this a funeral director is likely to arrive at someone's house probably with a removal vehicle when no death has occurred. I am sure that leaves little to the imagination as to the shock and distress such an experience can cause.

In Ken's early days as a funeral director he hired his hearse and limousines from a carriage master who ran his business from a small town not very far from Easingwold. According to Ken his vehicles were pretty ancient, which was not unusual in those days. The hearse he operated at that time had seen better days but was quite capable of doing the job provided it was on straight and level roads. However, any suggestion of an incline or, worse still, a hill, and then its performance began to deteriorate. Unfortunately Ken had a funeral in one of the hillier areas that surround Easingwold. They had left the family home and were driving in cortège to the church, which was several miles away for the funeral service and interment.

Midway between the house and the church was a rather steep hill. The driver said to Ken, 'I'll have to give it a bit of welly to get up here.' With that he put his foot down. Ken said there was a tremendous roar, something akin to a jet airliner taking off, as he attempted a run at the hill. They had very nearly reached the top when there was this noise which Ken said sounded like a gust of wind. He looked back over his shoulder and to his horror saw wreaths and sprays of flowers flying through the air, some landing on the road and others scattering into the fields. They had, until the sudden acceleration of the hearse, been on the flower rack which is on the roof of the hearse.

The driver did not stop until he had reached the summit and when he did he and Ken got out and so did some of the mourners from the cars in the cortège. Ken mumbled an apology and said he was going to retrieve the floral tributes from the road and the fields. Ken and the driver walked down the hill. The twenty-five or so wreaths and sprays were comparatively easy to find, but all that remained of them was the frame, the wire and the cards with the sender's inscription; not a petal remained. Anyway, they still collected them, returned to the hearse and proceeded to the church. Fortunately the main family flowers were on the coffin and remained intact. After the service they laid the flowers out in the churchyard so the family and friends were able to read the cards. Ken commented that it looked like a scene from Nagasaki. All Ken could do was tender his apologies and offer compensation.

I was never too keen on placing flowers on the roof of a hearse if travelling any distance; even with expanding restraints to hold them firmly in place there is always a risk of damage from the elements.

When we moved to our new premises in 1967 we were no longer able to leave the office unattended. The consequences of this was I began to spend a considerable amount of time at the office. I was soon arranging the majority of the funerals and my father was conducting them. That would not be the ideal way to proceed today as I am a firm believer in the funeral director meeting the family at the onset and remaining in personal touch with them through to the day of the funeral and beyond if necessary. It probably worked then because my father was so well known and his son making the arrangements did not seem to upset anyone. The problem was though that only my father and I could arrange funerals at that time. It was not until two or three years later that we had staff who could also arrange funerals.

By now my father was taking a holiday every year, which meant that when he was absent I was not only arranging the funerals I was conducting them as well. The problem was if I was away from the office for any length of time no funerals were being arranged. So we decided because of our excellent relationship with Ken Medd we would ask him if he would be prepared to conduct funerals on our behalf while my father was on holiday. This would also work when I was on holiday. Ken agreed and at a stroke this contributed to the efficiency of the business.

About this time Nigel, Ken's son, started a sort of apprenticeship with us, although that is not quite how Nigel described it. He seemed to think we asked him to do things that no one else wanted to do; of course that was ridiculous, we would never have done anything like that to a Medd. To use today's terminology he was involved in a learning curve. This meant that on occasions Ken as well as Nigel could be involved in our own funerals.

One such occasion was a funeral at Hinderwell, which is a village north of Whitby on the Yorkshire coast. For anyone who knows that part of the world they will be quite aware that it can blow a bit up there particularly in winter and this day was no exception. When the cortège arrived at the church, the gravedigger spoke to Arthur Carter who was driving the hearse and said, looking towards the churchyard, 'It's terrible up there, terrible.'

The wind was so strong that everyone had great difficulty keeping their feet, and as they proceeded into the churchyard where it was more exposed, the worse it became. Nigel described it as horizontal hailstones coming off the sea. By this time, Ken, who was conducting the funeral, had his head down so he was not getting the full force of the wind in his face. This unfortunately meant he was not looking in the direction in which he should be walking all the time; regrettably he strayed off the small path, tripped over a kerb which was surrounding a grave, hit the headstone and somersaulted over it, completely disappearing from sight.

Even though the bearers felt something akin to Captain Scott's party returning from the South Pole the sight of Ken as he vanished over the headstone was a little too much for them. Ken managed to recover and the interment took place. The end of the story bearing some resemblance to when I abandoned poor old Harry at that burial ground and the cow ate his hat. As it had been then, the first stop for Ken and party was the pub where a stiff drink was required to return their circulation to normal. Both Medds said that this was a Rymer set-up; rubbish, how could we possibly know what the weather would be like? Just the luck of the draw, I explained.

Ken had two brothers, Bob who was the eldest and John who is younger. Bob died some years ago. John is still fairly active but is mainly involved with the antiques side of the business. Back in the 1970s Ken had to spend some time in hospital. Bob and John looked after the funerals for this period, although John seemed to arrange and conduct most of them.

One Saturday afternoon they had a large funeral at a village nearby. It was summer but all the day it had looked as if we were going to have a thunderstorm. We had the service but as we came out of the church and into the churchyard for the interment the heavens opened. John, who was conducting the funeral, did not have an umbrella and was very soon drenched. The bearers, of whom I was one, got a little protection from the coffin, but not much and we were soon wet through. When we arrived at the grave we lifted the coffin off our shoulders with the help of Bob who was already at the grave and began to lower the coffin. Bob who had been at the head of the coffin appeared to still have hold of it and as the coffin began to disappear down the grave, Bob was going with it. Every second that went by I thought he would let go. By now he was on his knees beside the grave with his head and arms nearly out of sight. We were aware that something was wrong and had very nearly stopped lowering the coffin as one of Bob's arms was now quite visibly jerking backward and forwards. All of a sudden it came out of the grave along with the rest of Bob. He was soon on his feet and disappeared through the ring of mourners.

After the funeral we found Bob sheltering from the rain under a tree, although by now it was too late. He was obviously in some discomfort and his thumb had a blood-stained white handkerchief wrapped round it. Bob then explained what had happened. At each end of Medd's coffins they had a nickel ring which was screwed into the wood. Whether they had a use at any time I do not know, but now they were purely ornamental. Somehow as Bob was lifting the coffin off our shoulders his thumb had become wedged in the ring. At any other occasion than a funeral you would just shout stop, but Bob felt he could not do that and tried to extricate his thumb in silence. It was quite a mess and required stitches. Another example of a funeral director being involved in something above and beyond the call of duty.

One thing that can cause a problem for funeral directors is travelling in cortège from one city to another for the funeral, particularly if there is a considerable distance involved. The most difficult part is keeping the cortège together. In fact we have sometimes suggested to the family, especially if we were experiencing a period of inclement weather, that we would prefer to remove the deceased to another funeral director's chapel in the town or city in which the funeral is to take place maybe one or two days before. That funeral director will then conduct the funeral on our behalf. That way the family could make their own way and regardless of weather conditions or any other circumstances the funeral would be able to go ahead without fear of postponement, as has regrettably happened on at least one occasion that I can recall. It also means that this funeral director and his staff are working on familiar territory. But not every family will agree to this, insisting, quite flatteringly, that they wish the funeral director who by now they have come to know to conduct the complete funeral.

What all this is leading up to is something that happened to Ken Medd very soon after he started conducting funerals. He had to travel in cortège to a church that was in a town in the West Riding of Yorkshire. His hearse driver assured him he was familiar with the area and could drive straight to the church as he was sure he had been there before. Well he certainly got into the area and knew that the church was up a long lane leading from the main road. 'This is it,' he said confidently, and turned left into a lane and the cortège followed.

Unfortunately none of the mourners had ever visited the church before so they just followed the hearse. As they wound their way up the lane a scruffy handwritten sign appeared before them saying Joe's Scrapyard. There was no church, worse still there were no other turnings or space to turn round. They had no choice but to go into the scrapyard following a lane that was surrounded by scrapped cars, vans and other unrecognisable objects. They reached the top of the yard, where they were still unable to turn round. There only way out was to turn down another track that ran parallel with the one they had driven in on.

As they approached the gate there was a wooden hut, probably Joe's office. When they drew level with it a man stepped out of the door. It might even have been Joe; we will never know. His mouth dropped open and in an instant he removed his cap. Ken acknowledged his token of respect with a bow of the head. The cortège exited through the gate down the lane and eventually found the church. As far as Ken is aware the gentleman at the wooden hut was the only person to witness the incident. If so, would anyone believe him when he tried to explain to them that a flower bedecked hearse, complete with coffin and funeral director, closely followed by limousines with mourners had journeyed through his scrapyard that afternoon? Probably not. The moral of this story is, beware of hearse drivers who say they know where they are going.

Quite recently it was a case of history repeating itself. Nigel, Ken's son, was in the hearse that was in cortège for a funeral that was to take place in York. Nigel was giving directions to his hearse driver who was not too familiar with the route at that time.

Nigel said, 'Take the next turn left,' and before Nigel could stop him he did take the next left, but it was one road too soon and unfortunately it led directly into Tesco's supermarket.

'What do we do now, Nigel?' the hearse driver enquired.

'Follow the arrows,' Nigel said shaking his head. The look on the supermarket customers' faces was apparently something to behold as the cortège drove round the car park and finally back on to the main road.

Nigel has always had humorous names for his staff. An example is his hearse driver known as 'Jockey'. He also had two bearers he had christened 'Laurel and Hardy' for the obvious reason – they looked like them. But he had two bearers whom he did not have names for.

About two years ago Nigel had a funeral at a church which was to be followed by an interment in the churchyard. It was an appalling winter's day, snow was already several inches deep and a path had been cleared from the church to the graveside, but the snow was so heavy that whilst the service was proceeding the path was continually being kept clear. After the service the funeral procession emerged from the church and began to make its way to the graveside. They had not gone far when quite suddenly both pairs of legs of the bearers who were carrying at the head of the coffin just seemed to leave the ground and quite simultaneously they collapsed in a heap on the path.

I am happy to say that I have only seen bearers fall on two occasions, one whilst ascending church steps. In each instance they did not drop the coffin – almost as if some instinct tells them of the disastrous consequences of a coffin striking the ground no matter how well constructed. This has always been my main concern when volunteer bearers are involved in a funeral. If they trip they might just simply drop the coffin.

Nigel's two bearers were now laid on the path with the coffin on top of them. 'Laurel and Hardy' had managed to keep hold of their end of the coffin. Nigel, the minister and the family helped the bearers up on to their feet, along with the coffin – fortunately undamaged – and remarkably no one was hurt. They were able to proceed to the grave and the interment took place. Afterwards Nigel and his bearers inspected the place on the path where the fall occurred. It was an absolutely lethal area of sheet ice. When the minister, Nigel and 'Laurel and Hardy' had walked over it they must have just moved enough snow to expose the ice. When I spoke to Nigel some days later and he recalled the incident for me he said with a grin on his face that he had finally found names for the other two bearers to go along with 'Laurel and Hardy'. From now on they would be known as 'Torvill and Dean'.

Not long before Nigel bought his own hearse, our hearse was engaged for one of his funerals. As they were about to leave the house for the church they discovered the hearse would not start. The hearse driver and Nigel tried all they knew but to no avail. A replacement hearse was out of the question, as it was too far away. The options were a delayed funeral or somehow getting the hearse to church. After consultation with the family a rope was found and the hearse was towed to church where fortunately the interment was also to take place, so only one journey was required. The whole incident was less than dignified and Nigel who enjoyed finding alternative names for people and things found a new name for our hearse – I regret not printable.

Two of my staff were called to a house to remove a gentleman to our chapel. They rang the doorbell but got no response. After ringing again a voice called out, 'Come in!' They opened the door but no one was there. As they walked further into the house they shouted, 'Hullo!' A voice responded, 'Hello,' but still no one was there. Then the door of a room opened, a lady came out and was quite obviously startled to see our two men there. They quite hastily explained who they were and what had happened. Despite the circumstances, the lady had to smile and explained that the voice that had greeted them was her parrot.

Towards the end of my father's working life he was not too steady on his feet. I expect the most awkward places for him to conduct a funeral were churchyards where very often there are not proper paths to the graves and on more than one occasion he had been lucky to negotiate a safe passage there and back. One winter's day – incidentally, have you noticed how many of these events occur at this time of year – he had a funeral at All Saints' Church, Huntington, a village on the outskirts of York. As you leave the church for the interment in the churchyard you have to negotiate a sloping path. Yet again ice played a part but not such a disaster as Nigel's funeral. The minister led the procession followed by my father, the coffin and the family. As they started to descend the slope my father's foot began to slide and he was unable to stop. He appeared to pick up speed and very soon overtook the minister. By now the bearers said he was in quite a graceful glide his right hand in the air as if for balance. The left hand was clutching his black topper. As he approached the path on the left which led to the churchyard he seemed to indicate a willingness to turn but his momentum was too great and he continued down the main path, finally arriving at the lich-gate which acted almost like a buffer for a train. He very soon composed himself and made his way gingerly back to the procession.

Whilst I was recording this incident it reminded me of something that happened to me at this very same church yard many years before. I was one of the bearers carrying a coffin into the churchyard. It had rained quite heavily and the soil around the grave had become very soggy. When we arrived at the graveside we removed the coffin from our shoulders and two of us placed the coffin on the battens across the grave. I then attempted to move to my position to lower the coffin into the grave but my feet had by now sunk into the mud. What made it worse, my shoes were slip-ons and as I tried to extricate my feet I left my shoes behind and ended up lowering the coffin in my socks. Whether the family noticed I do not know. After the service I had to return to the grave and locate my shoes which by now had completely disappeared.

Just recently I was given a copy of one of our tabloid newspapers which had an account of a story with the heading, THE BLUNDERTAKERS. It told of a funeral where the cortège arrived late at the house and then travelled at great speed so that it would arrive on time for the funeral service. It also included reports of the family's distress. Now I am sure that in essence it was true. I am also aware that nothing in mitigation on behalf of the funeral director and his staff would be reported. Of course I do not know the background to this story so I cannot comment but all funeral directors, if they are completely honest, would have to confess to putting their foot down on some occasions so as to be able to keep to time. The ideal place to make up time is between funerals so the family are not involved.

There are many reasons why a funeral might run late and they are not necessarily all the funeral director's fault. One that would quite obviously be a funeral director's error would be arranging a funeral and not allowing enough time between it and the next funeral for the vehicles, staff and himself to arrive in good time. That should not happen, but can sometimes, particularly if a family have desperately wanted a funeral on a certain day and time. Your instinct is to say no, but you also genuinely want to do all you can for the family; yet if things go wrong, it might not be the family you are trying to help that will suffer. It may be the family of the deceased whose funeral will follow.

Other incidents that can cause delays which are out of the funeral director's control can be traffic, a breakdown, waiting for family or friends who have arrived late for a previous funeral; and then something that does not happen very often, thank goodness, is a minister who extends the time of his service at church well beyond its normal duration but neglects to inform the funeral director of his intentions, thus making it impossible for the funeral to arrive at the crematorium or cemetery for the committal service on time.

There are other circumstances that may cause delays but I think I have covered the most likely ones.

Before I leave this subject I must just recall another incident. We had arranged a funeral but the family wanted the cortège to leave from the deceased's house which had not been occupied for some time. The cortège arrived at the house on an estate on the outskirts of York. The funeral director went to the door and rang the bell. No reply – not even a parrot. After a few minutes the funeral director became concerned. Then a gentleman came out of a house opposite and asked what was happening. The funeral director explained that they were here for the funeral of the lady who used to live here. The gentleman very soon informed our funeral director that no such person had ever lived there. He returned to the hearse and checked his notes and then it dawned on him there was another avenue in another part of York with the same name. Had he got the wrong one? He was sure this was what had happened. The quickest way to get to the other address was via the York bypass, a distance of about thirteen miles. If the funeral was not to be late 'formula one' speed was required.

When they hit the bypass the hearse and three limousines would not have disgraced Frank William's, passing all other vehicles as if they were standing still. They were hardly late at all when they arrived at the house and were relieved to find the family waiting. It might not have been very dignified but at least the family were spared the distress of a late funeral. Having to drive fast or arriving late for a funeral is certainly no laughing matter but I have to say I think the name 'Blundertakers' is marvellous.

The majority of cemeteries and crematoriums are closed on Saturdays, so that only leaves private burial grounds and country churchyards where a funeral is possible at the weekend, and of course the majority of weddings take place on Saturdays, thus excluding a funeral service if required on the same day. But sometimes there are Saturday funerals. Some time ago we arranged a funeral which had to take place on a Saturday at a village church to be followed by an interment in another village churchyard about seven miles away. After all the arrangements had been made the family informed the funeral director that they would require six limousines to convey the family and friends from the church to the other village where the interment was to take place.

Now finding six limousines during the week can sometimes be a problem, but at the weekend very many funeral directors limousines' are engaged with weddings. We had three limousines at that time and two were unavailable because of weddings. So we began a search for another five. Our funeral director colleagues in York who had their own fleets could only let us have one each, that made three; we were able to acquire another limousine from a carriage master in a town nearby, that made four; but we were still two short and appeared to have run out of options. We contacted the family to confirm they still required six and they said they did. Under no circumstances did they want family or friends to drive their own cars in the funeral cortège.

I then remembered a carriage master in a town quite some miles from us who had from time to time hired vehicles from us. I had never seen his fleet but had been told that they were certainly not new vehicles. My funeral director had also heard that they might not be in exactly pristine condition and urged me to discover their true state if I was able to hire them. I telephoned Stan the proprietor and asked if he had two limousines available. I was delighted to hear he had. I then enquired what make they were and he told me, then almost apologetically I enquired as to their condition. I received what I was to discover in the years to come was a typical response from Stan. 'They're highly polished where there is no rust.' Thanks to Stan we obtained our six limousines and all went well.

All cemeteries and churchyards have the final say on any memorial that is to be erected. This has inevitably on occasions been the cause of a confrontation between families and the authorities. In some of the older cemeteries there have been erected some enormous memorials which would cost many thousands of pounds today. The main restriction is usually related to the height of the headstone and the prohibition of kerbs around the grave. That in my view is sensible. Without the kerbs it is considerably easier for the cemetery authorities to keep the graves tidy. There can also be constraints with regard to the inscription that a family have chosen for the headstone. Families find it difficult to understand why anyone other than themselves should determine the text and I must say I tend to agree, providing the inscription does not consist of anything that might cause offence, I see little reason to interfere. One of the most humorous inscriptions I have ever heard of was quite simply, 'I knew this would happen.'

Music at funerals has gradually changed over recent years. Maybe this is not quite so noticeable at churches, where traditional hymns are mainly sung, although sometimes even at church a family's personal choice of non-religious music is played. I am referring to music at a crematorium where a full funeral service is taking place and where the family appear to have more control of the content of the service. It is not unusual for the family to take their own tapes to the crematorium themselves. It is on these occasions that you are likely to hear quite a wide variety of un-funereal music.

I remember my father returning from a service at the crematorium one day and walking into the office. He exclaimed, 'I don't believe it – at the close of the service they had Frank Sinatra singing, "I did it my way".'

That was quite some years ago. Today it would not raise an eyebrow.

Among some of the more amusing songs we have had was, 'Wish me luck as you wave me goodbye' – nearly as good as singing 'Fight the good fight' at a wedding ceremony. But not so very long ago a song was played at a funeral which caused me to issue a new directive to my funeral directors. This was that ministers must be informed prior to the funeral if any music that could be termed unusual had been requested by the family at the crematorium service. I will explain. If the music is to be sung during the service the minister would have full knowledge of it. He quite probably will have discussed it on a visit to the family prior to the service. But if the music requested by the family is only to be played at the close of the service he would not necessarily know what had been selected. Towards the end of the service he depresses a button that indicates to the operator in the crematorium music room to commence the recording and on this occasion when he did press the button I think it is safe to say he was not prepared for what followed. It was Morecambe and Wise singing 'Give me sunshine'. As the minister left his lectern and walked past the catafalque curtains to the door that would lead him out of the chapel he almost seemed to be in tune with the music, and at any moment we expected to see his arms and legs simulate the famous duo.

Let me say that this is in no way a criticism of families selecting their own music and in some cases their own readings; anything at all that can make it easier and at the same time contribute to making them feel more relaxed must be encouraged at a funeral.

I know the heading 'Blundertakers' is meant to be funny but what of an account in a newspaper reporting improvements to a crematorium that is funny, but is not supposed to be. This appeared not so very long ago: 'Scarborough Crematorium will be given a warmer atmosphere after a decision to spend more than £27,000 on a new heating system!'

I hope I have been able to express in the previous pages how, even in our profession which experiences much tragedy and heartache, there can sometimes be room for a little humour without any loss of dignity, respect or professionalism. I have seen it help families and friends and it can certainly contribute in making the funeral director's and his colleagues' work a little more light-hearted.

Chapter Seventeen

What I have endeavoured to relate in the previous pages is in part a story about a family where the men have been funeral directors continuously ever since that day in 1854 when James Rymer made the decision to arrange and conduct the funeral of his daughter, Margaret. Men of course played the prominent role but the business would not have succeeded without the vital contribution of the wives, daughters and sisters in the family. I am sure that through the years many of the ladies were involved with the administration, along with other tasks that would assist the business; but even before telephones arrived their main contribution was just being present at the place of business, which in our case was the home as well.

In those early days when someone died, and it was nearly always at home, a member of the family would just come along, knock on the door and expect someone to answer. I know people did not have holidays in those days but my family just like anyone else would have liked to close the door and all go out together, maybe to visit family or friends or just simply for a walk, but that was never possible; someone always had to be there. Nothing has changed today. When someone dies, especially at home, they do not want to wait for attention, nor should they; but until the advent of the telephone diverter, and for us that was in the early 1980s, someone had to be there.

With the diverter we devised a rota with each funeral director being on duty for a week. Each evening at 5 p.m.

and at the weekend the telephone is diverted to his home so he receives any calls direct. Of course their wives or partners are still vital to this procedure; while the funeral director is attending a call she must remain at home to answer any subsequent enquiries. Some funeral directors may have a mobile telephone which enables them to be contacted while on the move, thus shortening the time factor. I am not sure about answerphones; they will not suit in my view a large funeral director, who will be receiving many calls, and he certainly cannot afford to be absent for any long period of time. Maybe a much smaller business can just get away with it if they return to their machine frequently. My own analysis of telephone answering machines is that most people prefer not to speak to them, even for private calls; but when someone has died to have to convey that distressing message to a machine is just too much.

I am often asked what changes have taken place over the years in our profession. Well, there is one thing that has not changed; someone has always to be there on the end of a telephone. Of the changes that stand out to me, I would mention not making our own coffins, lady funeral directors and women in general playing a much larger role in the profession. Family and friends taking part in funeral services and the advent of the funeral plans, being able to pre-arrange and pay for your own funeral.

You cannot talk about changes in our profession without referring to the cost of funerals. They, like everything else, have increased over recent years but funerals much less so than many other commodities. Yet whenever the media spotlight falls on our profession it is a safe bet that the cost of funerals will be included. There was one gentleman who used to turn up on programmes frequently and appeared to have such a dislike and distrust of funeral directors, particularly with regard to their charges, that I am sure if we offered him or a member of his family a free funeral, a three-course meal afterwards for everyone who attended the funeral, plus two weeks in Tenerife, I am convinced he would still think we were all crooks.

Sometimes we are asked for a 'simple' funeral. It is important that funeral directors define what the family mean. They are unlikely to mean a low cost funeral but they probably want a funeral with very little ceremony, unadorned and unpretentious but, at the same time, with no loss of quality of service, dignity and respect.

Another big change over the last forty years is the gradual disappearance of some of the small funeral directors, although many still remain. For instance the NAFD membership of funeral directors in York in 1955 was twenty-one; today only two of those original members remain. There have in recent years been many mergers and acquisitions and consequently some large groups have emerged. The biggest of these is SCI UK (Service Corporation International), originally a family firm established as Heights Funeral Home in Houston, Texas, in 1962 and now the largest funeral service company in the world. My old firms were originally part of the Plantsbrook Group but are now part of SCI and I am a Consultant Director. In many ways this can be quite awesome when you have been used to operating a much smaller business.

Prior to the acquisition I had several meetings with Peter Hindley, who is now Chief Executive Officer of SCI UK, and James Brown, the Managing Director. They both held corresponding positions at Plantsbrook. It was made clear to me that they in no way wished to interfere in the traditional manner and customs in which the business was run or to change the staff and management. What they pledged to do was enhance the highest standards of service, to expand the selection and quality of merchandise and commit sufficient capital to develop the funeral directors' premises. All this has been done starting with a £150,000 refurbishment of our main offices and chapel. They place much emphasis on education and have a national training director; these are things that we could never have provided, certainly not at that level, so all in all we have derived many benefits ourselves and the public also receives a higher quality of service. The most important thing is that the Rymer family still operate the business. When circumstances necessitate a change of staff we still carry out the applicant interviews ourselves so we can hopefully retain the consistency of the character and personality of personnel who have been employed at J. Rymer over many years.

When a company such as SCI takes over your business, regardless of any assurance or pledge that might be made prior to the acquisition, in theory they can do as they like, but Peter and James are very much aware of the personal nature of our profession and its local customs. Any major change, or in some instance just minor 'tinkering', could quite possibly reduce the public's confidence in that business. This is not SCI's way and it did not happen. They currently spend one million pounds per annum in staff training and in 1997, £3,500,000 was allocated to funeral premises and crematoria refurbishment. Quite simply their aspiration is to have the most highly professional staff working within the most prestigious premises providing an unrivalled quality of service. What a pity business success can often attract unreasonable carping and it does.

J. Rymer has been a member of NAFD, the National Association of Funeral Directors, for nearly seventy years; it appears my father joined the then BUA, British Undertakers' Association, which was founded in 1905 very soon after my grandfather's death in 1925.

The Association changed its title in 1935 and although there are others the NAFD is the largest of our trade associations. It has had its ups and downs in recent years but I fervently believe it provides a solid base for our profession and ensures the public gets a fair deal. The head office was based in London until 1989, when it transferred to Solihull. It has its code of practice, encourages and promotes education for its members and their staff and twice a year holds examinations for the Diploma in Funeral Directing. It has done its best to assist members face changing demands and in answering criticisms of the industry, including some damaging allegations, much of them ill-informed. Today it is aligned with many groups and organisations which are allied to our profession, holding joint meetings and seminars and making a genuine effort to help everyone it can.

My father sent me to my first local NAFD meeting when I was about eighteen. The venue was a room below ground level in an old building in the centre of York. In those days a certain amount of animosity still existed between some members, making for a new member an unfriendly atmosphere. My feeling as I left that first meeting was that I was in no hurry to attend the second. Eventually I did start to attend the meetings with my friend Ken Medd, the funeral director whose exploits I have recalled earlier. With an effort from both of us the meetings began to liven up. We suggested a new venue and soon our meetings were taking place at The Black Swan on Peasholm Green, one of York's oldest pubs dating back to the four-teenth century. Almost at once it changed the whole atmosphere, but our numbers were small so we decided to have a recruitment drive for new members. I was probably in the best position to approach funeral directors as we supplied quite a number, mostly in the rural areas, with vehicles. Several expressed an interest and we held a meeting and meal at a local hotel so they could meet up with the existing members. The evening was a success and the majority who were there that evening agreed to join the Association.

In 1968 I was elected President of the York Branch; Ken was my Vice-President and succeeded me the following year. My father then encouraged me to attend the Yorkshire area meetings, which I did accompanied by Ken, and in the later years with Ray Garbutt and some of the other York members. In 1985, Andrew Waite invited me to join the public relations team that represented the Yorkshire area and in 1987 I was elected to the Yorkshire area Executive Committee and in 1989 had the honour of becoming the first York funeral director to be elected the Yorkshire Area President. In 1990 I was elected Chairman of the Yorkshire Funeral Vehicles Owners section of the NAFD which specialises in transport matters within the profession. When it was formed in 1946 I think most of its members would have been solely carriage masters, and although there are some of them left the membership today consists mainly of funeral directors and carriage masters combined. The meetings are always well attended and the section is run, as it has been for many years, extremely efficiently by its secretary, Betty Naylor.

The NAFD has had its ups and downs and in 1994 it had a real down. To be fair, there had been some discontent within the membership for some time. Then some large groupings resigned. Unfortunately Plantsbrook was one of these and included my business. This ended an association that went back nearly seventy years and I was very sorry. It also meant that I had to resign the positions I held in the NAFD, including my seat on the Yorkshire Executive committee and my public relations position, and of course I was unable to attend any meetings. However, within a year, SCI were in control and we were back inside the NAFD.

In my view the NAFD have been very fortunate to have had some very competent people on the National Executive at nearly all the crucial times, particularly when the boat was rocking; and it still remains in my view by far the most trusted organisation to represent our profession now and in the future. Its main aim must surely be to convince as many funeral directors as possible from large groups, medium-size firms to one-man bands to either join or rejoin the Association. I have been asked whether I am optimistic or pessimistic about the future of our profession. Well, I have to be optimistic, there is an increased professionalism among the majority of funeral directors today. Of course, there will always be one or two 'cowboys' who will let the others down, but they are few and far between and if they are members of the NAFD we should catch up with them.

There are only one or two aspects of the work that I am concerned about; one that I have touched on earlier is counselling, or the over-reliance on counselling and I am not just referring to counselling for the bereaved but counselling in general. Some time ago I listened to an edition of the radio programme 'In the Psychiatrist's Chair'. The subject was Martin Bell, the BBC's foreign correspondent and now an Independent MP. He was responding to Professor Anthony Clare's questions on his experiences, particularly in circumstances when he was in extreme danger. He was shot on one occasion, and as we know journalists and cameramen have died following their vocations, but he had also witnessed many times the appalling and tragic aftermath of insurgence and war and was asked how he came to terms with such experiences and did he require stress counsellors. I have not got Mr Bell's exact response but the gist of it was that stress counsellors had not been there. He wanted to be self-reliant and if he felt the need to talk to anyone at all it would be, in his words, 'with my mates'.

I think this reiterates what I have said previously about counselling, that there may be occasions when a professional counsellor is required but the comfort of family and friends is paramount.

I have also commented earlier on police press conferences where bereaved relatives are paraded in front of the media. The *Daily Mail* columnist Lynda Lee-Potter commented recently about this very topic describing how a fifteen year old child had been subjected to this ordeal after the murder of her friend. Miss Lee-Potter summed up my own reaction completely by stating, 'It's obscene to expose people who are almost crazed with grief and since these ghoulish affairs never produce worthwhile results it is time they were stopped.'

I do not feel I have to apologise for these criticisms of counselling and police press conferences because I have been very close to people for well over thirty years who have experienced the most tragic bereavements and I think I know what I am talking about. Of course things move on, and much of what is new is good, but I doubt very much if the basic needs of a family experiencing a bereavement have changed, or the manner with which they cope with it. I have acquired over many years of conversation with relatives a certain amount of medical knowledge. How very often have I listened to the exact same account of someone's last illness and eventual demise, of things that were done and things that should have been done, and have thought to myself, I will remember that but as some wise person once said, 'A little knowledge is a dangerous thing.' I would probably end up putting two and two together and getting five. If you know what I mean.

Some years ago I had a conversation with Richard Thompson, who had a joinery business based in a village near York. Richard was the grandson of Jim Wentworth who was the village funeral director there for many years and we used to supply him with hearses and limousines. After a break of some years Richard began to arrange and conduct funerals himself. I will always remember him saying to me one day, 'I do not want to be doing this job that long that I end up arranging the funerals of my friends.' Now I know many funeral directors will not feel that way. I was a few years younger than Richard but I wholeheartedly agreed with him.

When Richard died and I attended his funeral service I remembered what he had said and realised that I was fast arriving at that position myself. I carried on for some time and did indeed arrange funerals of friends during that period. At the start of 1995, although I had told no one, I had decided that this would be my last year as a funeral director. Though I was happy to remain as the consultant I did not want to be involved on a day-to-day basis. In the summer of 1995 I arranged a funeral with a family I knew and decided that was it.

I still spend some time at the office each week and give advice and help when required to our staff and anyone else who cares to ask. My sons now run the business and the majority of the staff are of a similar age to them. I feel that they have freedom to do things their way without me there. How often has someone hung around too long and impeded the progress of a business? They already do some things in a different way, although I am not sure whether everything they do is an improvement, but from time to time every business benefits from a facelift. If I had still been there every day they maybe would not have tried anything new and I might have been guilty of restraining a good idea.

I wonder what old James Rymer would have thought of it all today. It is a hundred years since he died and some things have not changed. As in his day, funeral services are still held in the York city churches followed by an interment at the old York Cemetery opened in 1837. One thing we know for sure he never arranged a cremation service and most probably knew very little about it, although the first crematorium in this country was opened at Woking in 1885, thirteen years before his death. What would he have thought of lady priests, lady funeral directors or mass-produced coffins? Could he possibly have envisaged the cost of funerals today and the disappearance, thankfully, of the pauper funeral? And I very much doubt he ever had two mourners attending a funeral in handcuffs along with prison guards, as we had recently. I think it unlikely that a Victorian prison governor would have permitted such a compassionate gesture.

I have always been a little surprised how little my father seemed to have known about James Rymer; this was probably because my grandfather died when my father was only fifteen and he had not got round to relating to him the family history. If I recall correctly I was turned twenty before I began to take any real interest in who had preceded me. However, we did know why James came to York and how he became a funeral director; but we had virtually nothing personal about him other than my father said someone had once described him when he was turned eighty as being 'tall and erect' – bearing in mind that not many people managed to live until their mid-eighties one hundred years ago.

In September, 1996, we arranged and conducted the funeral of a Mrs Edith Jackson, aged 98 years. After the funeral I received a letter, as we very often do, thanking the funeral director and his staff for the efficient funeral arrangements. Included with the letter was a lengthy postscript from Mrs Jackson's son, Peter. He informed us that our firm have been arranging and conducting funerals for his family for over ninety years and that his family were living in St Andrewgate when James Rymer was still in charge of the business.

I telephoned Peter Jackson and made an appointment to meet him and his wife so I could talk personally to him about James. When I met Peter, he told me that his mother, Edith, was the daughter of James and Jane Booth who in 1883 lived at 41, St Andrewgate. The business was run from premises at 35, St Andrewgate, from 1848 until 1967. Jane Booth (Peter's grandmother) was often employed by James to lay people out at their homes, we refer to it as the last offices. I do not know what family James had around him in his final days but Peter remembers his grandmother telling them that she sat with James during his last nights and subsequently laid him out after his demise.

She described him as 'a very hard man' and 'an old skin-flint' but at the same time highly respected for the sympathetic and efficient way in which he treated his customers. Jane went on to describe how on James's bedhead was a line of hooks. On the hooks were hung small leather pouches in which he kept his money. In the evenings when Jane was sat at the foot of his bed he would lift each pouch down in turn and proceed to count the contents. Each pouch contained twenty-five gold sovereigns and he counted them every night, even on the night of his death. Peter asked me not to take offence as he had only related the story as his grandmother had told it. I said we had survived worse names than 'skinflint'. On the night he died Jane was sitting in his room and decided to poke some life into the fire in the bedroom fireplace. As she did so a bright red glow lit up the back of the fireplace.

James sat upright in bed and declared, 'It's Old Nick,' and then lay down again. I sincerely hope it was not a premonition. Those are the only words we know for sure the founder of our firm actually said. Jane carried on working for the firm up until and throughout the First World War and for some years afterwards. In 1938 Jane and her family moved away from St Andrewgate to another area of York and she died in 1951, aged 89 years. Rymers of course carrying out the funeral arrangements.

Peter Jackson has a beautifully documented photographic history of St Andrewgate which he has titled, 'The story of a street'. After seeing it I think he must be St Andrewgate's unofficial historian. I am extremely grateful to him for relating the story about my great-great-grandfather just in time to include in this book. Although I did not meet Peter's sister I would also like to thank her, as she has also contributed to these reminiscences.

I have heard it said that being a funeral director is a calling. Well, that may be so but in my case if it was I have no recollection of the call. I went into the business because I wanted out of the Royal Marines School of Music and it seemed the lesser of two evils. In those early years in the business helping make coffins in the workshop, cleaning cars and being a bearer I had no real responsibility nor did I want any. I did not like the job and thought that one day some time in the future I would be doing something else. I think the turning point for me was my father's first holiday in 1961. Although I had help it was my first real responsibility. In 1964, my mother and father visited the USA and Canada for two weeks. Very soon after they returned home my father went into hospital to have a cataract removed. When he eventually returned to work I had been running the business on my own for a month; the corner had been turned. I never ever became completely used to being a funeral director, but when arranging and conducting a funeral concentrated everything into making sure the family got the funeral they had chosen. I was always extremely gratified when people took the trouble to thank me, either by newspaper acknowledgement, verbally or by letter. I also began to build up a great respect for the profession. I believe we have a funeral service second to none in this country, along with all the many other people who contribute to the funeral arrangements.

In 1984 a letter arrived at the office advertising the sale of an illustrated dictionary. Normally my father would disregard such things but I remember him saying distinctly, 'We had better have that.' When it arrived it was in two volumes A–K and L–Z. Whilst writing this book I have referred to them many times to ensure that I had chosen the correct word or to confirm my proper use of fixed phrases and inflections. Other than looking at them when they arrived, I do not recall my father ever referring to them. However, I have many times over the years, particularly when I had my job in public relations. As I have been writing this book I have almost had a feeling my father was saying, I told you I knew this would come in handy some day.

Well, that is about it. I have tried to relate a story about a family of funeral directors along with everything and everybody that is connected to this profession. If my peers think I have left anything or anybody out, I apologise. If anything I have written proves to be controversial or I have offended anyone, I am sorry but cannot apologise for my opinions. I often wonder how many of the funeral directors I have met over the years were not so terribly enthusiastic about their job. After all, many of them were only in the business because it had been passed down through the family, exactly the same as myself. If they were they managed to disguise it. I however started out a reluctant funeral director and after all these years nothing has changed – I still am.